The Multi-Instrumental Guitarist
BANJO · MANDOLIN · UKE · DOBRO® · DULCIMER

The Acoustic Musician's Guide to Versatility

Alfred, the leader in educational publishing, and the National Guitar Workshop, one of America's finest guitar schools, have joined forces to bring you the best, most progressive educational tools possible. We hope you will enjoy this book and encourage you to look for other fine products from Alfred and the National Guitar Workshop.

Copyright © MMII by Alfred Publishing Co., Inc.
All rights reserved. Printed in USA.
ISBN 0-7390-2813-8 (Book and CD)

This book was acquired, edited and produced by Workshop Arts, Inc., the publishing arm of the National Guitar Workshop.
Nathaniel Gunod, acquisitions and editor
Michael Rodman, editor
Matt Cramer, music typesetter
Tim Phelps, interior design
CD recorded at Castle Acoustics in Knoxville, KY, and Bar None Studio in Northford, CT

Guitar photo: courtesy of Gibson U.S.A.
Resonator guitar photo: courtesy of Fender Musical Instruments
Mandolin photo: Weber Fern Mandolin, courtesy of Sound to Earth, Ltd. © Rob Outlaw
Ukulele photo: courtesy of C. F. Martin & Co.
Lap dulcimer photo: Timmy Abell

GREG HORNE
WITH STACY PHILLIPS

TABLE OF CONTENTS

About the Authors 4
Introduction 5
How to Learn Folk Music 6
Chapter 1—Mandolin 8
   Meet the Mandolin 8
   What to Look For 8
   Assume the Position 9
   Mandolin Tuning 10
   Open Chords 11
   Shuffling Away 11
      Boil Them Cabbage Down 11
   Movable Chords 12
   More Chords 13
   The Almighty Chop—It's All in the Wrist 14
      Eight Bars Does Not a Prison Make 15
   Mandolin Fingering 16
   The Two-String Major Scale 16
   Playing Melodies on the Mandolin 18
      Soldier's Joy 19
   Harmonies and Drones on Adjacent Strings 20
      Variation on Soldier's Joy A Section 20
   Unison Slides 21
      Old Joe Clark 21
   Blues, Mando-Style 22
      Bluey for Louie 22
   A Blues Scale for Blues Leads 22
      Bluey for Louie Solo 23
   Rock 'n' Roll Mandolin 24
      The Ballad of Excelsior Jones 24
      The Improved Ballad of Excelsior Jones 24
      The Solo on the Improved Ballad of Excelsior Jones 25
Chapter 2—The "Octave Mandolin" Group: Octave Mandolin,
        Irish Bouzouki, Irish Tenor Banjo 26
   Octave Mandolin Tuning 27
   Chords 27
   Movable Chord Shapes 27
   Irish Ornaments 28
      Drowsy Maggie 29
   Playing Jigs 30
      Scatter the Mud (Chords and Rhythm) 31
   Jig Melodies 32
      Scatter the Mud (Melody) 33
Chapter 3—Tenor Banjo and Tenor Guitar Swing and Dixieland 34
   Tenor Guitar Tuning 34
   Open Chords 35
   Movable Chords 35
   Lead Tenor Banjo/Guitar 36
   Dixieland Rhythm Style 36
      When the Saints Go Marching In 37
Chapter 4—Introducing the Five-String Banjo 38
   The Happiest Instrument Known to Humanity 38
   What to Look For 38
   Some Handy Devices 39
   5-String Banjo Tuning 39
   Notes on the Banjo in G Tuning 39
   Holding the Banjo 40
   Open Chords in G Tuning 40
      Boil Them Cabbage Down (Chords Only) 40
   A Tale of Two Banjos 41
Chapter 5—Banjo: Clawhammer Style 42
   The Clawhammer Technique 42
   Frailing, the Brushstroke, or "Bump-Ditty-Boom-Chicka" 43
      Boil Them Cabbage Down (Basic Clawhammer) 44
   Hammer-ons and Pull-offs 44
      Pull-Off Your Hammer-On Stay Awhile 44
      Old Joe Clark (Simple Clawhammer) 45
   Drop Thumb, or "Melodic" Clawhammer 46
      Old Joe Clark (Melodic Clawhammer) 47

    Modal Tuning 48
        Shady Grove 49
    C Tuning 50
    Basic Chords in C Tuning 50
        Soldier's Joy 51

Chapter 6—Banjo: Three-Finger Style 52
    Fingerpicks 52
    Three Basic Banjo Rolls 52
        Boil Them Cabbage Down into Cabbage Rolls 53
        Cripple Creek 55
    Backup Banjo 56
        Sittin' on Top of the World (Backup Banjo) 57
    Putting the Blues in Your Bluegrass 58
        Sittin' on Top of the World (Lead Banjo) 59
    Kickoffs and Tags 60
    Single-String Style Banjo 62
        Béla Notey 63
    Melodic Banjo 63
        Simple Gifts (Low Octave) 64
        Simple Gifts (High Octave) 65
    Rock 'n' Roll Banjo 66
        The Ballad of Excelsior Jones (Rolling Banjo) 66
        The Ballad of Excelsior Jones (Melodic Banjo) 67

Chapter 7—Ukulele 68
    Ukulele Tuning 68
    Open Chords 69
    Movable Chords 69
    Strumming 69
    Old Time Banjo Uke 70
        Soldier's Joy with Old-Time "Wakachicka" Strum 70
    Advanced Uke 71
        Ukulele Boogaloola 71

Chapter 8—Baritone Uke and Tenor Guitar (Guitar Tuning) 72
    Baritone Uke and Tenor Guitar Tuning 72
    Open Chords 72
    Movable Chords 73
        (No Better Sweater Than) Laura's Angora 73

Chapter 9—Lap Dulcimer 74
    Mixolydian Tuning and the Mixolydian Mode 74
    Frettin' and Strummin' 75
        Over the Waterfall 75
    Dulcimer as a Modal Instrument 76
        Rock That Cradle, Joe (Melody on the A String) 76
    Advanced Dulcimer Playing 77
        Rock That Cradle, Joe (Melody on the D String) 77

Chapter 10—Lap Slide Guitar 78
    Types of Slide Guitars 78
    G Major Tuning (High Bass G Tuning) 79
    Strings for Playing Lap Slide 80
    The Right Hand 80
    Bars (Slides) 81
    Basic Left-Hand Technique 82
    Playing the "Strumming Blues in D" 83
        Strumming Blues in D 84
    Single-String Technique and Scale Patterns 85
    Playing "Country Blues in G" 86
        Country Blues in G 86
    Double Stops and Vibrato 87
        Double Stop Piece 88
    Playing "Blues Shuffle in E" 89
        Blues Shuffle in E 90
    Working with Chords 91
    Open D Tuning 92
        Piece in Open D 93

Summary of Tunings 94

ABOUT THE AUTHORS

Greg Horne is a performer, writer, producer and teacher. He holds a Bachelor of Arts in Music from the College of Wooster, and pursued graduate studies at the University of Mississippi's Center for the Study of Southern Culture. Greg has been an instructor at the National Guitar Workshop's summer campuses since 1990, specializing in songwriting and acoustic courses. He is the author of *The Complete Acoustic Guitar Method*, also published by the National Guitar Workshop and Alfred. Greg has produced several albums of his own songs, as well as producing and performing on projects for other writers and bands. He lives in Knoxville, Tennessee, where he writes books and songs and tries to decide which instrument he should be practicing next. For more information, go to www.greghornemusic.com.

Greg wrote Chapters 1–9 of this book.

Stacy Phillips is an internationally acclaimed lap steel guitarist and violinist. He has recorded and/or performed with Leon Redbone, Eileen Ivers (from Riverdance), Peter Rowan, Bela Fleck and Mark O'Connor. He is a featured performer on the 1995 Grammy award-winning album The Great Dobro Sessions.

Stacy performs in many styles including jazz, klezmer, Hawaiian and bluegrass. He is also the author of over 25 books and videos on various aspects of violin and steel guitar. He has conducted workshops in schools throughout the world.

For more information, go to www.stacyphillips.com

Stacy wrote Chapter 10 of this book.

Interior photography of Greg Horne and instruments Chapters 1–9 by John Black. Interior photography Chapter 10 by Tim Phelps.

A compact disc is included with this book. This disc can make learning with the book easier and more enjoyable. The symbol shown at the left appears next to every example that is on the CD. Use the CD to help ensure that you're capturing the feel of the examples, interpreting the rhythms correctly, and so on. The track number below the symbol corresponds directly to the example you want to hear.

INTRODUCTION

Welcome to *The Multi-Instrumental Guitarist*. Learning new instruments is a wonderful way to break out of a rut. In addition, the minute you begin learning a new instrument, you learn new things about music that will improve your playing on every other instrument you play. This book will introduce you to several popular instruments that are related to the guitar in their playing technique: mandolin, octave mandolin, bazouki, tenor banjo, five-string banjo, ukulele, baritone uke, lap dulcimer and lap slide guitar (Dobro®, resophonic slide guitar). Most of the instruments covered in this book come from the folk, swing, blues and bluegrass traditions of America and the Celtic tradition.

WHO SHOULD USE THIS BOOK
This book is designed for intermediate guitarists. However, intermediate players of other fretted string instruments should not have much trouble getting around this book. It assumes that you are comfortable with the following skills and knowledge:

- Tuning the guitar (or other fretted string instrument) in standard tuning
- Reading tablature (TAB) and chord diagrams
- Reading and playing strum rhythms and chord changes
- Playing barre chords and some scales
- Playing with a pick (some fingerstyle techniques are included, but experience is not necessary)
- Understanding of the chromatic scale (the music alphabet with sharps and flats)
- Understanding of the major scale, major keys, and simple chord structures such as major, minor and 7th chords

In addition, it will be helpful if you are familiar with the 12-bar blues form and pentatonic scales. You do not need to read music to benefit from this book, though music notation is supplied for most of the examples. If you need to catch up on the basics, try *Beginning Acoustic Guitar*, also published by the National Guitar Workshop and Alfred.

HOW TO USE THIS BOOK
Each instrument has its own chapter. Some chapters may apply to several instruments that are tuned the same way. Each chapter starts off with the basics of tuning and technique, and then goes more in depth. Even if you don't have access to all the instruments in this book, read through the chapters. Many songs and techniques can be translated from one instrument to another. Some instruments can even use the same TAB and chords as others.

Before you start, make sure to read "How to Learn Folk Music" on page 6.

WHICH INSTRUMENT SHOULD I BUY FIRST? WHICH IS EASIEST TO PLAY?
The answers to these questions are different for every player. Just follow your instinct and try things out. Borrow from friends or rent from a local store. Learning one instrument makes the next one easier, even if they are as different as banjo and lap steel. Here are a few tips:

Mandolins and ukes are relatively inexpensive to start out on, and easy to carry around. Five-string banjos allow you to try two totally different fingerpicking techniques, and you can also tune up the four low strings to play tenor banjo music. Four-string guitars or banjos have great possibilities. With just one of these instruments, a good tuner and a variety of string gauges, you can check out music ranging from ragtime tenor to Irish bouzouki. Lap slide instruments are totally addictive for blues and Hawaiian music, and will guarantee that you're not just "one more guitar" at a jam.

This book is dedicated to Jim Turley, who so kindly introduced me to "old-time" music, and to the memory of John Hartford, who made me want to play everything I heard him play.–G.H.

Special thanks to David Lovett and the staff of Pick'N'Grin for the use of their instruments.

HOW TO LEARN FOLK MUSIC

The last twenty years have seen an explosion in written material available for all kinds of instruments. The Internet and video have made it possible to get instruction on just about anything you can think of. Books and other materials are valuable ways to learn new instruments, particularly if you don't have access to teachers.

The music in this book is based on several folk music traditions. Folk music is considered an oral tradition. This means that the method of learning was traditionally from the mouth of one person to the ears of another. With musical instruments, a better term might be an "aural tradition." In the days before mass media (most of the days of human history, in fact) an aspiring musician would sit at the feet of an elder player, watching and listening with the focus of a dog on a tennis ball, then run home and try to do the same thing.

Even now, there is no teacher of folk music like observing and playing music with other people who have mastered an instrument or style. There are nuances of sound and touch that are different from region to region, county to county, and person to person. You will add your own stamp to the tradition when you play music with others.

HOW TO LEARN TUNES THE WRONG WAY
To get the most out of a book on folk music, blues, or jazz you must slightly alter your approach to the book. When you read music in a book, your instinct will be to try to play the whole tune, to "find out what happens next." As you reach a certain level of proficiency, you can indeed do this.

However, beginners often find that after they work on a tune long enough to figure it out, they are then "stuck" to the book. In other words, they have become proficient at reading the tune from the book, instead of playing the tune. When they encounter variations on the tune from other players, it can be confusing and frustrating. Remember, folk music and improvisational music like blues and jazz are fluid, living traditions. Everybody has a different version of a tune, but most of them will fit together one way or another!

HOW TO LEARN TUNES THE RIGHT WAY
Think about the goal of learning a tune. It may be to play with others, or just to have a new tune to play yourself. The important thing is to learn the tune by heart. You don't want to be dependent on your music books in a jam session. Folk music requires you to be flexible, quick to adapt, and above all to have fun! If you know one or two tunes really well, you will have more fun than halfway knowing twenty. As you go along, you may be able to pick up new songs by just hearing them. This is because you can hear the similarities and differences between the new tunes and those you know from memory.

LEARN IN SMALL "BLOCKS," AND GET AWAY FROM THE WRITTEN MUSIC AS SOON AS POSSIBLE!

To take full advantage of the limited time you have to practice, try this technique when learning folk music:

1. Look through the music to **get an idea of the basic "shape" of the melody**, as well as the structure of the tune. If you can, listen to the tune several times, both while looking at the music and without the music. Try to hum or sing along. The more the melody gets in your ear through singing, the easier it will be to know if you are playing it right. Old-timers call this process "setting the tune in your head."

2. Begin at the start of the tune and **work on just a small "block" of information**. This may be as small as one move or one beat, or as much as a bar or phrase. Most folk music is made up of tiny melodic ideas and moves. Many of these little "blocks" occur over and over again as you learn new songs. They just combine and recombine in different ways like atoms and molecules. Be aware that as you learn one tune, some of the same moves may appear in many other tunes. The hard work you do now will pay off tenfold!

3. **Start memorizing** right away. Play your tiny "block" over and over (and over and over) without looking at the music. Check back occasionally to make sure you've got it right, but then go back to playing it from memory.

4. **Work on the next block.** When you have it down, go back and attach it to the first block to make a bigger block. Think of those little plastic blocks kids play with: Two small blocks stick together to make one big one. Pretty soon the kid's built a space city with a working monorail and sustainable power grid. And all you want to do is to play a 16-bar fiddle tune!

5. Go back and play your old tunes *often*! This is called "**repertoire building**." You need to build your collection of tunes, then make sure they stay dusted off and roadworthy. You never know when you might need to jam "sCripple Creek" one more time.

This process may seem like the "slow" way to learn a tune, but actually it is the fast way. If you learn just one or two bars of music a day, you can learn a new tune every week. One year and you've got fifty tunes by heart (or five tunes on ten instruments, you pickin' fool, you), with two weeks off for summer bluegrass festivals.

GET OUT AND PLAY
Folk music is meant to be shared, like conversation, food and love. Don't be afraid to get out and play. Just pay attention to what other people are doing and try to match them, even if it's only for one session. Every tradition deserves respect. Good luck and remember to have fun!

CHAPTER 1
MANDOLIN

MEET THE MANDOLIN

The mandolin is a great extra instrument for the guitarist. Since it is played with a pick, you don't have to learn an entirely new right-hand technique to play it. If you have any background with violin or fiddle, the mandolin will be even easier. It is basically the left hand of a violin (with frets) with the right hand of a guitar.

Here are the pieces and parts of the mandolin.

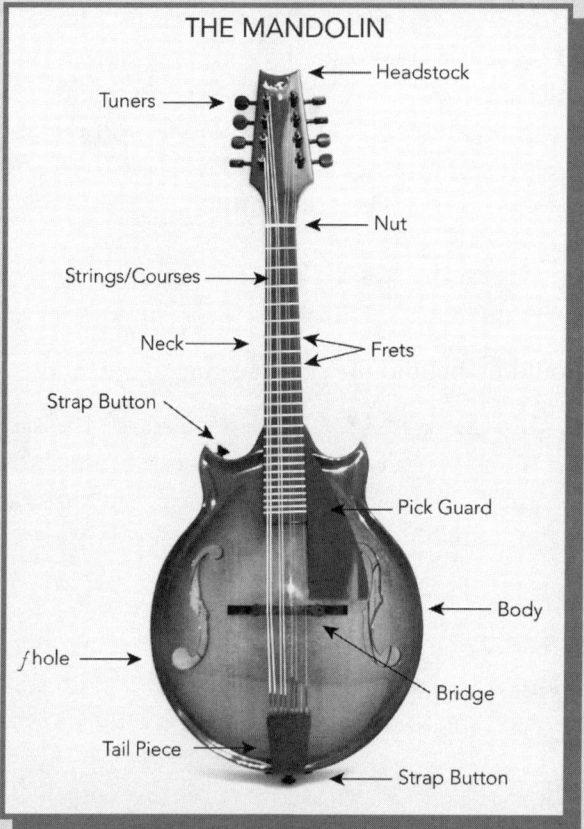

WHAT TO LOOK FOR

There are two popular styles of mandolin models plus many variations. The two basic styles are based on the Gibson company's most popular models, the "A" and the "F," which were designed in the early 20th century. A-style mandolins are generally teardrop shaped, and may have *F-holes* (holes that are roughly in the shape of the letter F, like on a violin) or an oval-shaped soundhole. Many F-style mandolins have a scroll on the upper bout and F-holes. Both styles can sound great. You should look for a mandolin that has a straight neck, comfortable action, working tuners, and no sinking spots in the top. Solid-wood instruments will generally sound richer than plywood instruments, but will cost more. If it sounds good and is easy to play, go for it.

> **MULTI-INSTRUMENTAL MADNESS:**
> If you are looking for more music to play on the mandolin when you finish this chapter, try the examples in the Irish Bouzouki/Octave Mandolin chapter (page 26). The written music and the tablature are the same, they just sound an octave lower when played on bouzouki or octave mandolin. The fingerings will be a bit different, however, due to the longer scale length of those instruments.

ASSUME THE POSITION

When it comes to holding the instrument, you have a couple of choices. You can use a strap, attached at the endpin and at a strap button on the upper bout (or looped around the headstock). The strap may go over your head (around your neck) or over one shoulder. Some players hold the mandolin to their body with their right forearm, but this can restrict movement and cramp your muscles.

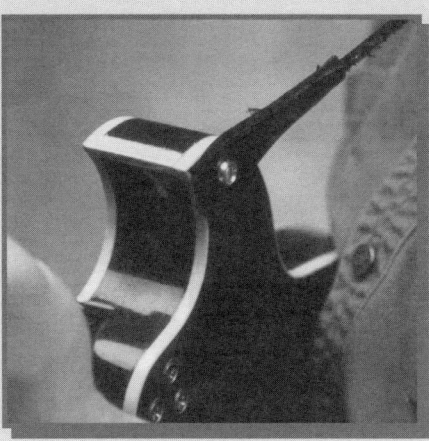

Looped *Buttoned*

Your left-hand thumb should be behind the neck, resting lightly and allowing the palm to be open. Sometimes, you may need some extra leverage, which may require you to squeeze with both your thumb and the palm of your hand. Try not to bend your wrist sharply either forward or backward. Stay relaxed!

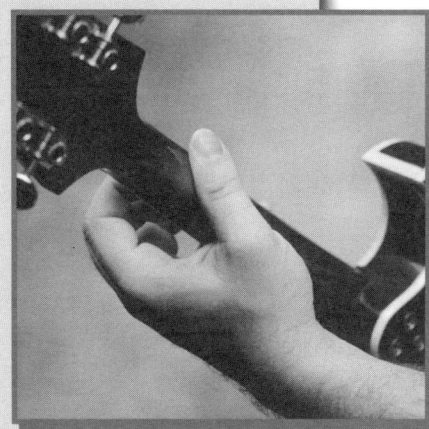

Thumb behind neck

Mike Marshall's *touring and recording career began as a member of the original David Grisman Quintet in 1979. Since those days Mike has been at the center of the acoustic music scene and can be heard on hundreds of recordings of acoustic music. His mastery of mandolin, guitar and violin and his ability to swing gracefully between jazz, classical, bluegrass and Latin styles is rare in the world of American vernacular instrumentalists. He has performed and recorded with some of the top acoustic string instrumentalists in the world including Stephane Grappelli, Mark O'Connor, Béla Fleck, Edgar Meyer, Montreux and Joshua Bell.*

In 1986 Mike founded a classical string quartet of mandolin family instruments (two mandolins, mandola and mandocello). This group, the Modern Mandolin Quartet, released four recordings for Windham Hill Records, which redefined the mandolin in a classical music setting. In 1995 the Quartet made its Carnegie Hall debut and in 1996 received a "Meet the Composer" grant from the Lila Wallace Foundation.

MANDOLIN TUNING

The mandolin is tuned identically to the violin. It has eight strings, arranged in four *courses* (sets of strings), tuned in *unisons* (each pair of strings is tuned to the same pitch). If you are used to reading guitar music, you will notice that the mandolin notes sound higher at the same pitch than the guitar notes. This is because the guitar music actually sounds an octave lower than written. Mandolin notes sound exactly as written.

The mandolin is tuned in 5ths. This means that the strings are a perfect 5th, or seven half steps, apart. The example below shows the tuning of the open strings (each course is identified as one string on the TAB), and the frets you would use to match them on lower, adjacent courses.

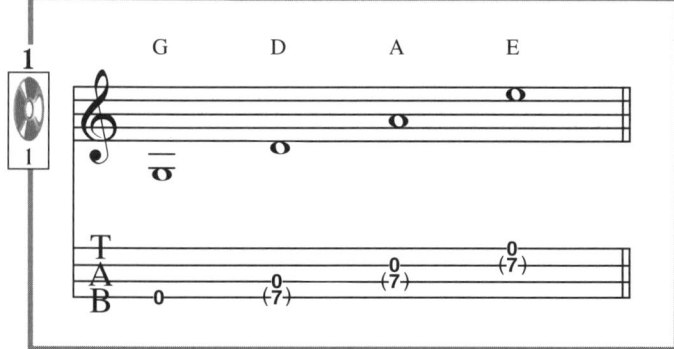

You can tune your mandolin to Track 1 of the CD.

You can use the CD for this book, a guitar tuner, a chromatic tuner or a pitch pipe to get a reference tone for one string, then tune the other strings to it. For example, if you first tune a string of the 4th course to G, follow this procedure.

1. Match the unisons of the 4th course.
2. Tune an open 3rd string to the 7th fret of the 4th string. Match the unisons of the 3rd course.
3. Tune an open 2nd string to the 7th fret of the 3rd course. Match the unisons of the 2nd course.
4. Tune an open 1st string to the 7th fret of the 2nd string. Match the unisons of the 1st course.

Here is a diagram of the entire mandolin neck, with all the notes marked.

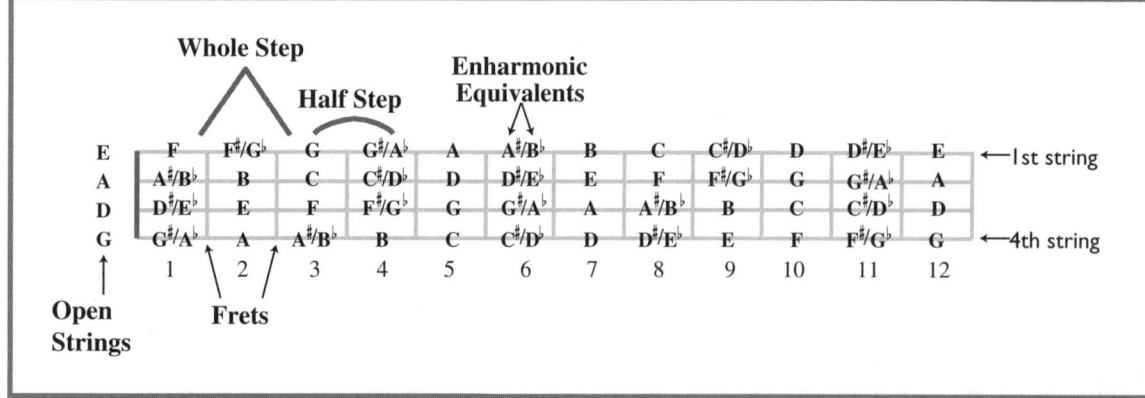

GUITARISTS BEWARE:
The dots on the mandolin fingerboard tend to be placed at the 3rd, 5th, 7th, 10th and 12th frets. This can be confusing if you're used to seeing a dot at the 9th fret.

OPEN CHORDS

Following are some basic chords to use on the mandolin. Use the left-hand fingers indicated above the diagrams.

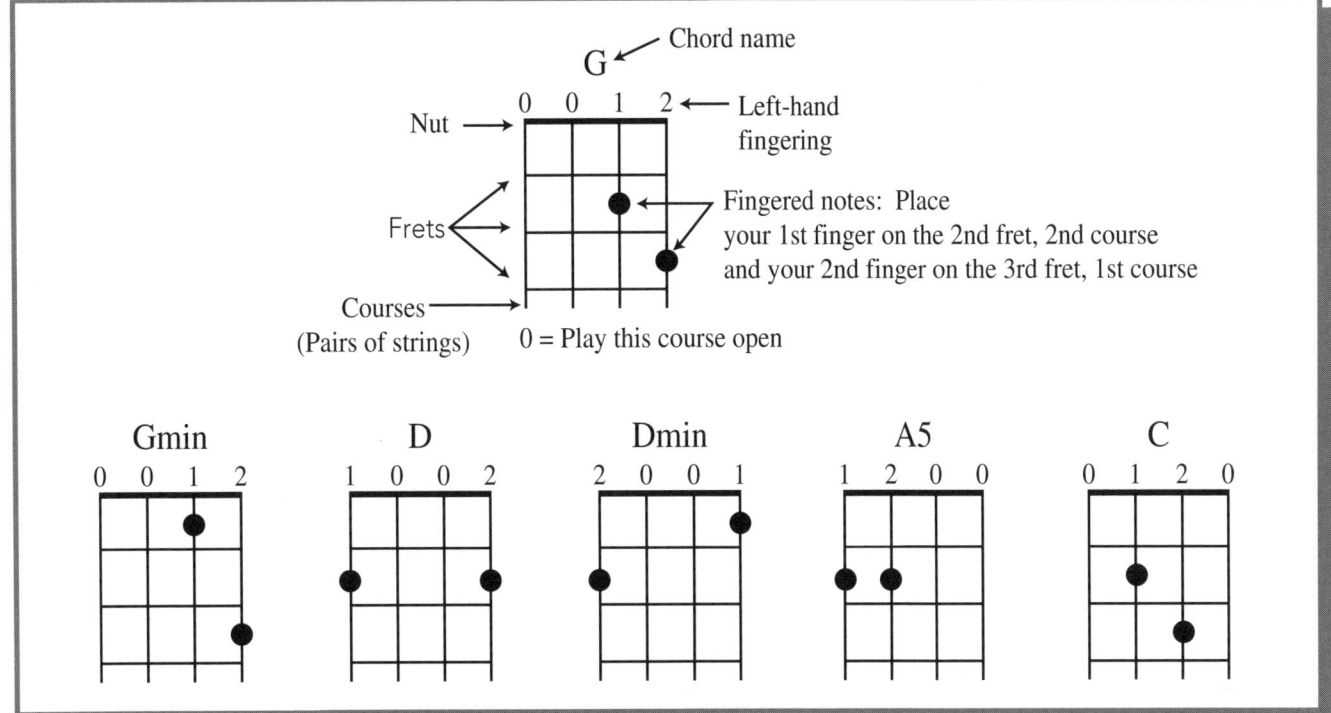

SHUFFLING AWAY

Try these chords with this song, first using simple downstrokes. Then try the simple strumming rhythm indicated. This rhythmic pattern mimics the "shuffle" rhythm heard in bluegrass and old-time fiddling. In fiddle and bluegrass terminology, "shuffle"* refers to a quarter/two-eighths rhythm (or an eighth/two sixteenths). This makes the "dumdiddy, dumdiddy, dumdiddy" sound that underlies a lot of fiddle bowing and mandolin picking. This song is an old Appalachian classic, and sounds much better than boiled cabbage smells.

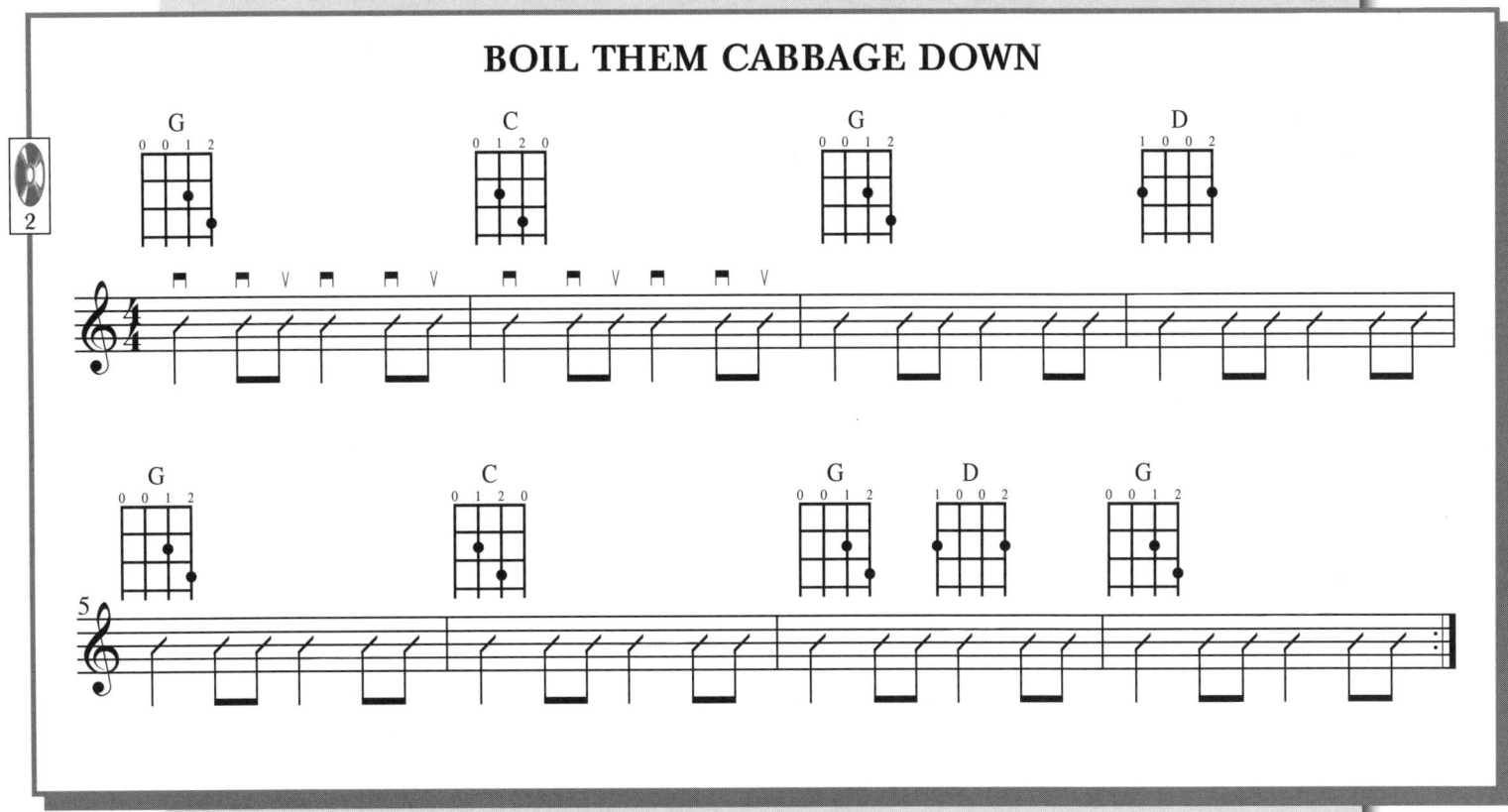

* The term "shuffle" is sometimes used by blues musicians to describe a "swing" rhythm, where eighth notes are played unevenly. The word does not have this meaning in bluegrass terminology.

MOVABLE CHORDS

Since the mandolin is tuned in 5ths, and only has four courses, there aren't that many chord shapes to learn. Following are some movable chord forms. The roots have been noted on the diagrams using a letter "R." To find any chord you might need, locate the root you want, and then build the chord shape using the fingerings indicated.

MOVABLE CHORD FINGERING NO.1
This fingering is used heavily in bluegrass rhythm playing, because the notes of the chord are *voiced* (arranged) fairly close together. This provides more density and punch to the voicing. Note that this voicing can have its root on the 3rd string for a four-note version of the fingerings or the 4th string for a three-note version. Both major and minor fingerings are shown.

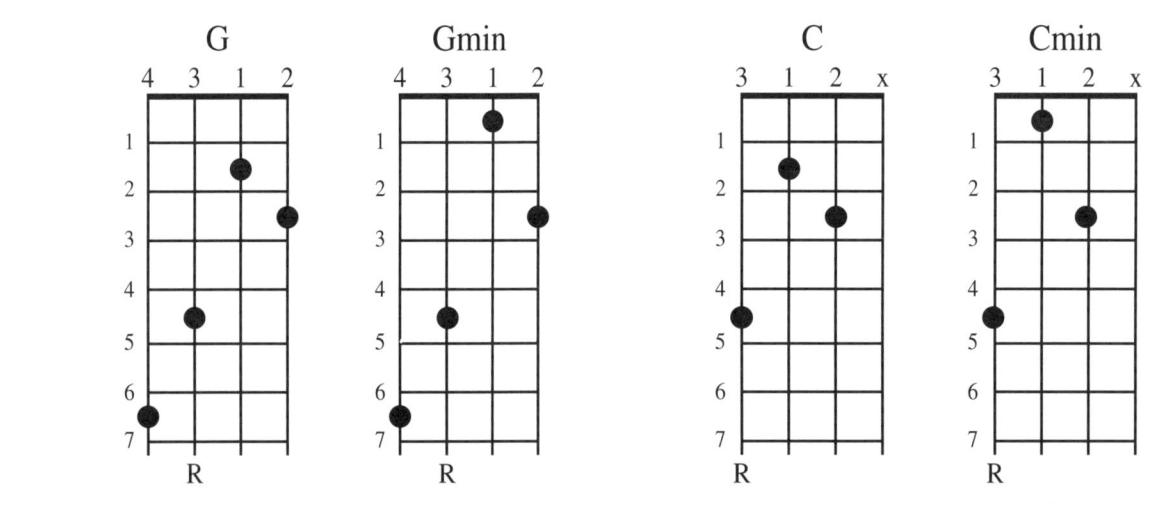

MOVABLE CHORD FINGERING NO.2
This is a more open-sounding voicing. Note that it is based on the open "G" chord you learned on page 11. It is very easy to finger both the major and minor versions of this voicing. It is also easy to add a 7th to the voicing.

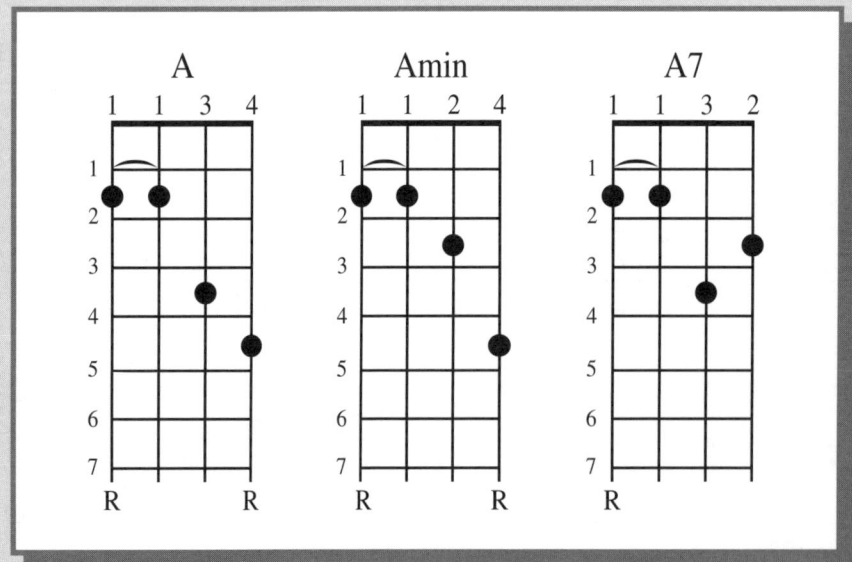

12 • The Multi-Instrumental Guitarist

MOVABLE CHORD FINGERING NO.3
This fingering is based on the open "D" chord you learned on page 11. This one is also easy to finger in both major and minor voicings.

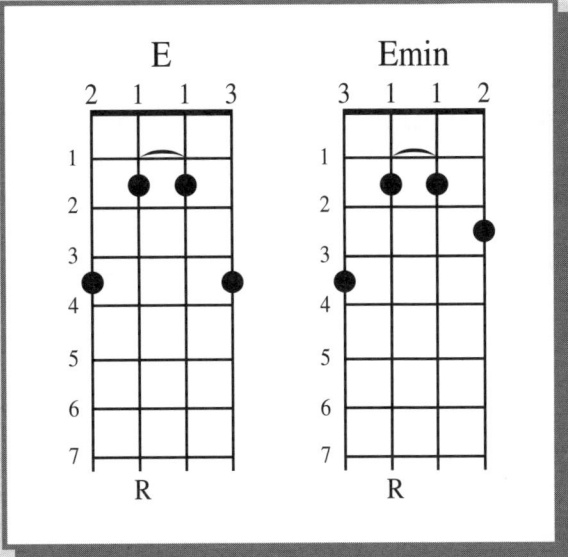

MORE CHORDS

Here are some 7th chords and other handy voicings based on the movable shapes you have learned.

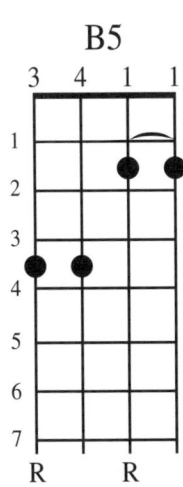 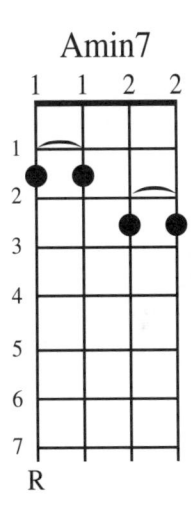 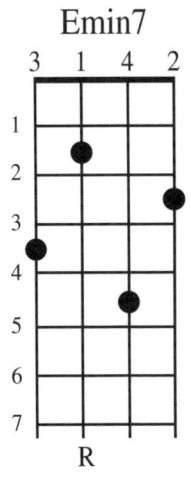 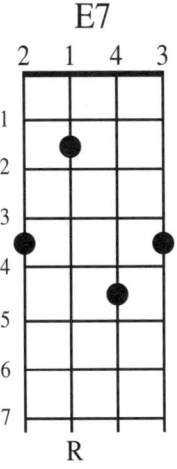

The Multi-Instrumental Guitarist • 13

THE ALMIGHTY CHOP—IT'S ALL IN THE WRIST

The mandolin sounds great when strummed with ringing open chords or with individually picked arpeggio patterns. However, the most famous sound of the mandolin in American music is the short, percussive, rifle-shot *chop* heard in bluegrass. Using the chop sound on beats two and four, the bluegrass mandolinist joins in a melding of the minds with the bass player (who plays on beats one and three) to form a single, unified rhythm section.

While the chop can be played with open chords and some creative string muting, it is easiest to use the movable chord forms that have no open strings. The sound is made by fingering the chord, strumming it with a brisk flip of the wrist downward (a downstroke), then immediately relaxing the left-hand fingers, keeping them on the strings, to cut off the notes. The more you use the weight of your right hand and flick your wrist, the more percussive the sound. Try the chop using a G Major chord as shown.

Sometimes, you will want to very simply chop on beats two and four as shown above. However, it is easier to get a groove going if you add a couple of extra elements. Many bluegrass players will add a quiet downstroke on the 4th string on beats one and three. This creates a "boom-chick-boom-chick" kind of strum that you may be familiar with from country and bluegrass guitar playing. Here's the trick: play the "boom" note softly, and hold the chord until you've "chopped" it on beat two. Try this pattern using a G and C chord.

14 • The Multi-Instrumental Guitarist

You can also add upstrokes to your strum. Now that your hand is moving in a steady beat throughout the measure, you can throw in an upstroke every now and then to *syncopate* the rhythm (shift the accent to a weak beat or weak part of the beat), making it "move" more. Try this bluegrass progression.

EIGHT BARS DOES NOT A PRISON MAKE

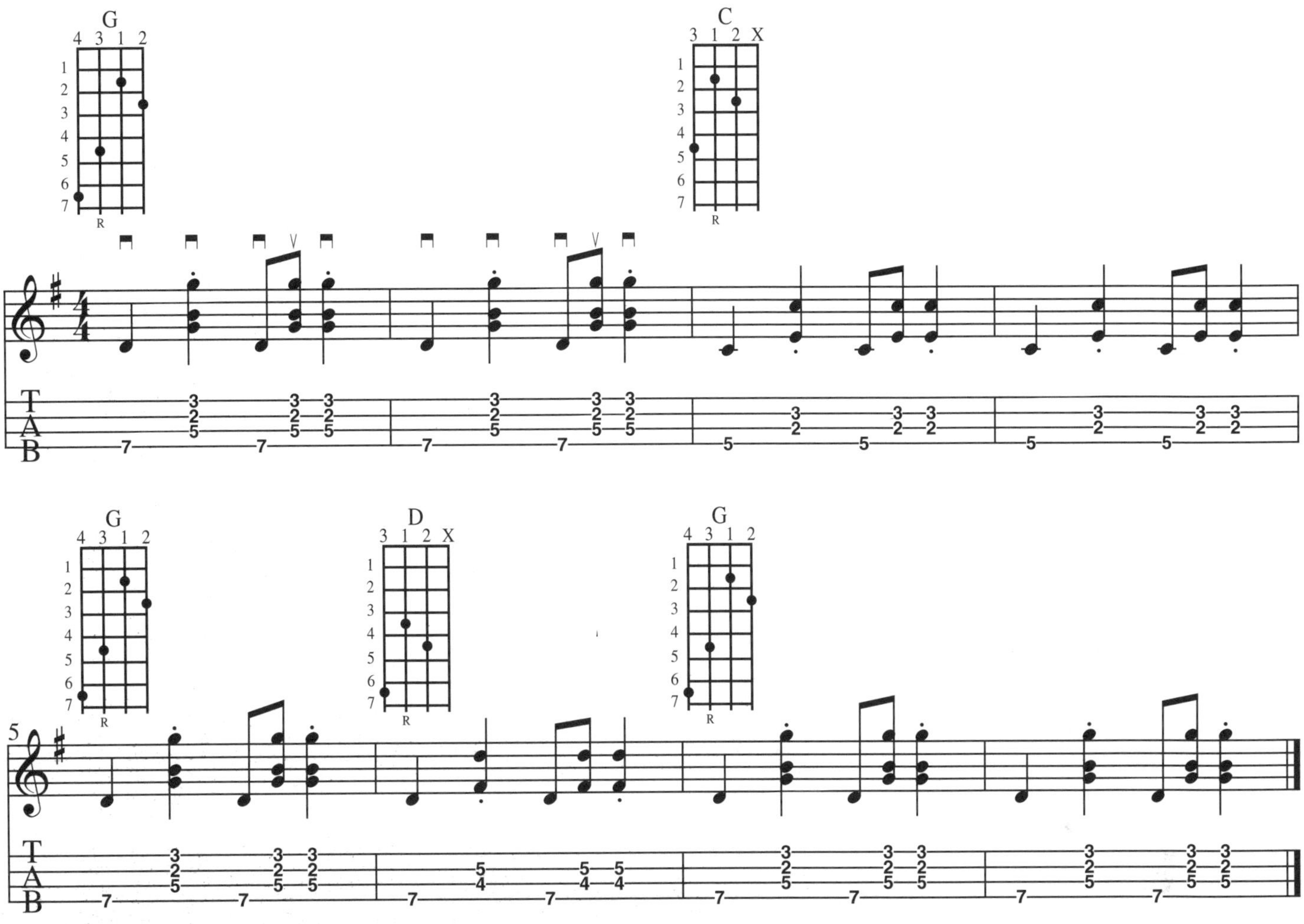

PHOTO • MAUREEN DELGROSSO

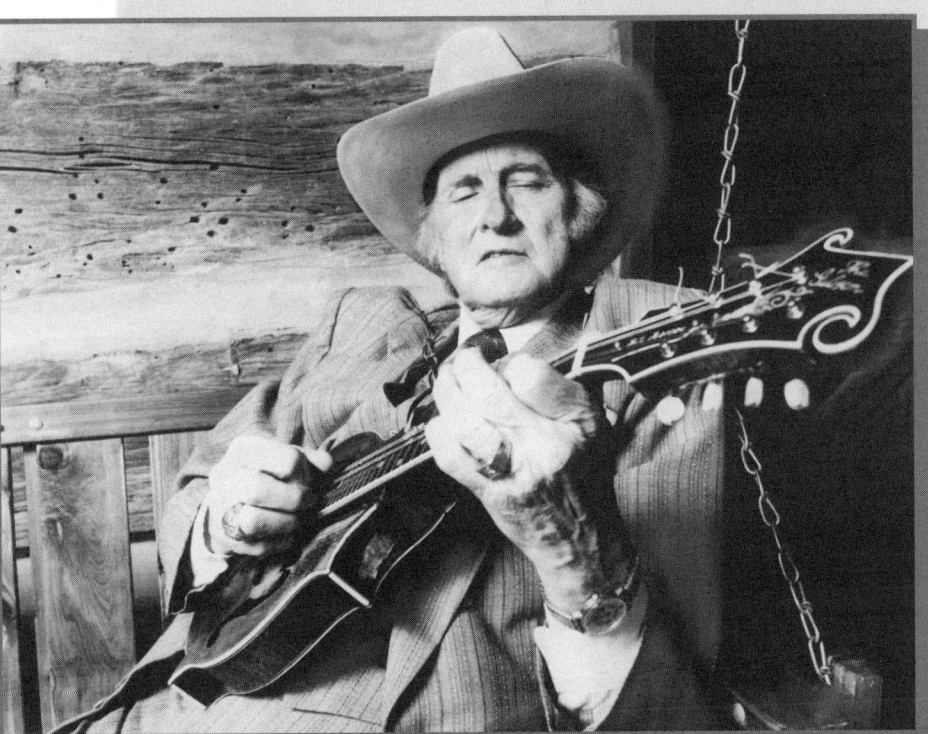

***Bill Monroe** (1911-1996), the "Father of Bluegrass," defined the bluegrass mandolin style for many players who came after him. In addition to his classic solos and great rhythm playing, he was one of America's great songwriters.*

MANDOLIN FINGERING

You will notice the greatest difference between the technique of the mandolin and that of the guitar when fingering scales and melodies. Due to the longer scale length of the guitar, we generally use one finger per fret to form a "position" on the fretboard. On the mandolin, the left-hand fingering is similar to a violin, with the fingers stretching out over a position including six to seven frets.

Here is how it works for each finger in the open position, depending on the scale and key:

Left-Hand Finger	Frets Played
1st Finger	1st or 2nd fret.
2nd Finger	3rd or 4th fret. The 2nd finger may be held so that it touches the 1st finger or 3rd finger, depending on which frets are being used.
3rd Finger	5th or 6th fret. The 3rd finger may also be used to slide up to the 7th fret.
4th Finger	6th or 7th fret.

Left-hand fingering

THE TWO-STRING MAJOR SCALE

Below is a D Major scale shown on two strings. Note that your 2nd and 3rd finger may touch each other to help solidify the position. For a review of the structure of the major scale, the *whole steps* (two frets) and *half steps* (one fret) have been indicated.

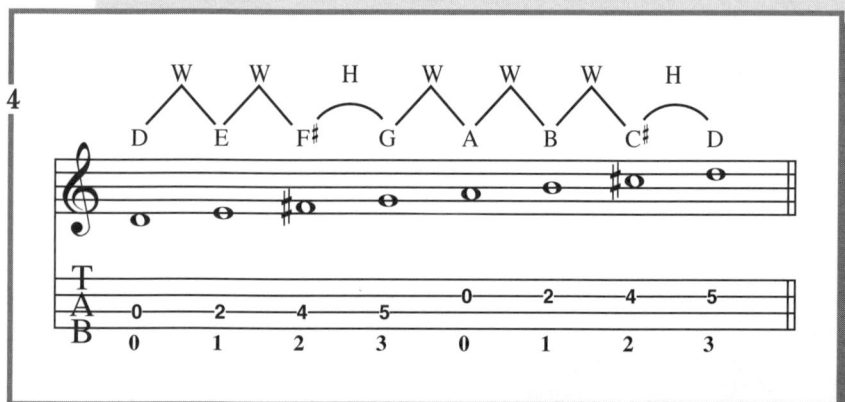

W = Whole Step

H = Half Step

The open position major scales on the mandolin (G, D and A) are very easy to work with because the fingering stays the same on both strings. Unlike the guitar, the smaller mandolin allows you to easily finger four scale notes per string.

D MAJOR SCALE

Here is the full D Major scale in open position. The key notes, or tonics, have been highlighted.

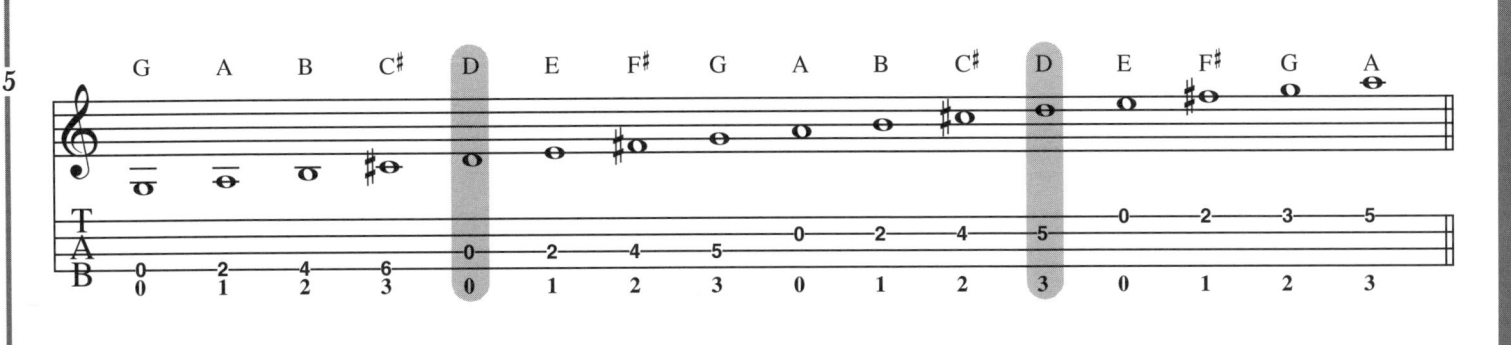

G MAJOR SCALE

Here is a full G scale in open position. Note that the fingering is the same as a D Major scale shifted down one string. You can use this scale to play lead mandolin on songs in the key of G Major. Try improvising over the progression of "Eight Bars Does Not a Prison Make" (page 15).

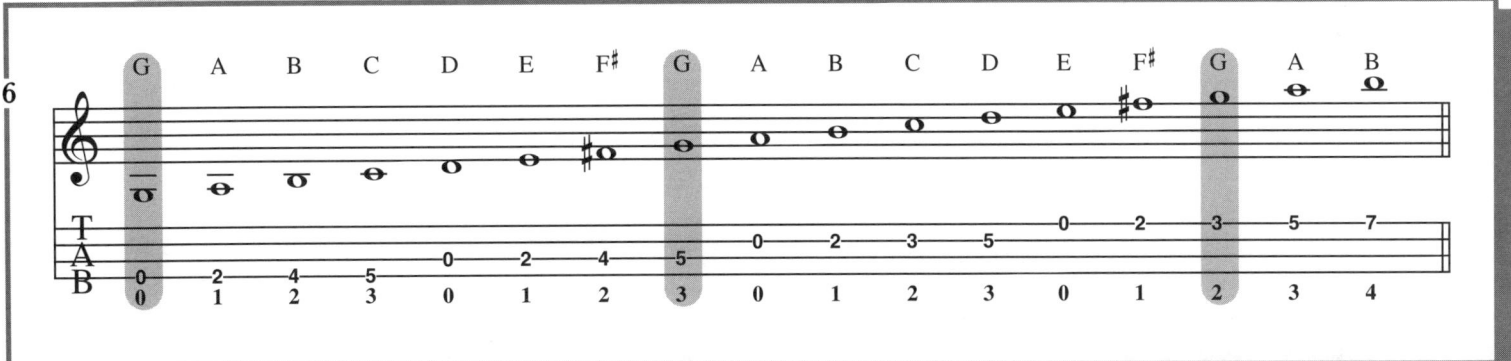

Yank Rachell (1910-1997) was one of the most prolific and influential blues mandolinists playing both electric and acoustic mandolins. His performing and recording career spanned seven decades and included work as a soloist and with artists such as Sonny Boy Williamson and Sleepy John Estes.

PHOTO • MAUREEN DELGROSSO

PLAYING MELODIES ON THE MANDOLIN

Much bluegrass, old-time and *Celtic* music (the traditional music of the Celtic countries: Ireland, Scotland, Wales, Brittany, etc.) is based on fiddle tunes used for dancing. These tunes are overwhelmingly played in the common major keys of D, A, G and C. The version of "Soldier's Joy" on page 19 will help you start your collection of tunes in the key of D Major.

ALTERNATE PICKING

Alternate picking (or "down-up" picking) is crucial to developing the speed and agility you will need for this music. It is important to develop a consistent approach that locks in with the basic pulse of the song. Use downstrokes for all onbeats (counted with numbers 1, 2, 3, 4) and upstrokes for offbeats (counted on the "and" between the numbered beats). Also, make sure to hit both strings in a course with each downstroke or upstroke of the pick!

Try these exercises.   V = Upstroke.

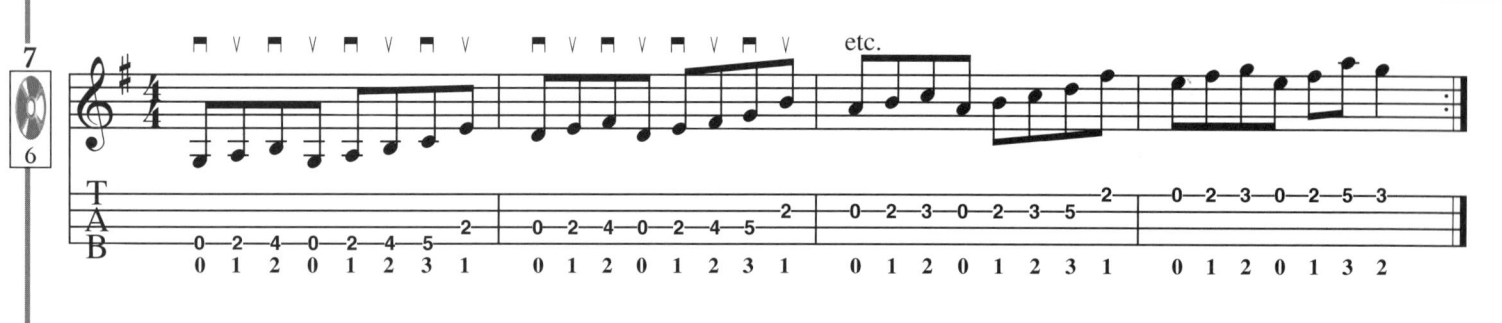

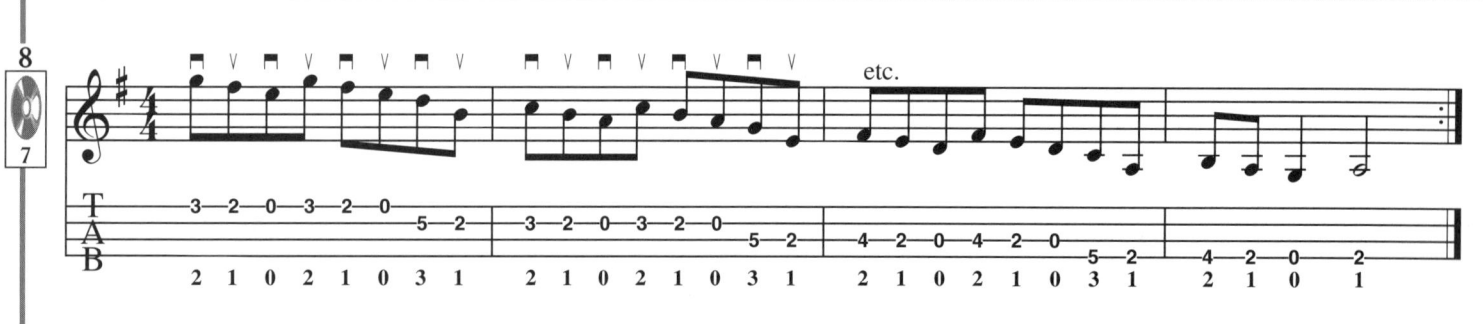

The following tune is a favorite at old-time and bluegrass jams. It is an old fiddle tune played in the key of D Major. Learning fiddle tunes is a great way to build your jam repertoire and develop your chops as a lead player. Like most fiddle tunes used for dancing, this one has two parts (called the "A section" and the "B section"). Each part must be played twice, as the repeats indicate.

JAMMING TIP:
Always learn the chords of jamming tunes, as well as the melody. Practice your rhythm playing so that you can provide a solid foundation for someone else. Otherwise, you'll be no fun at a jam session!

18 • The Multi-Instrumental Guitarist

SOLDIER'S JOY

HARMONIES AND DRONES ON ADJACENT STRINGS

As you have learned, the mandolin is very closely related to the fiddle. An integral part of the Appalachian fiddle sound is the use of harmony notes and drone notes on strings adjacent to the melody string. For example, a melodic passage played in the key of D Major on the 3rd string may be played against the open 2nd string. Since the A note on the 2nd string is part of a D Major chord, it will blend with much of the harmony implied by the melody notes. Try this variation on the A section (first two lines) of "Soldier's Joy."

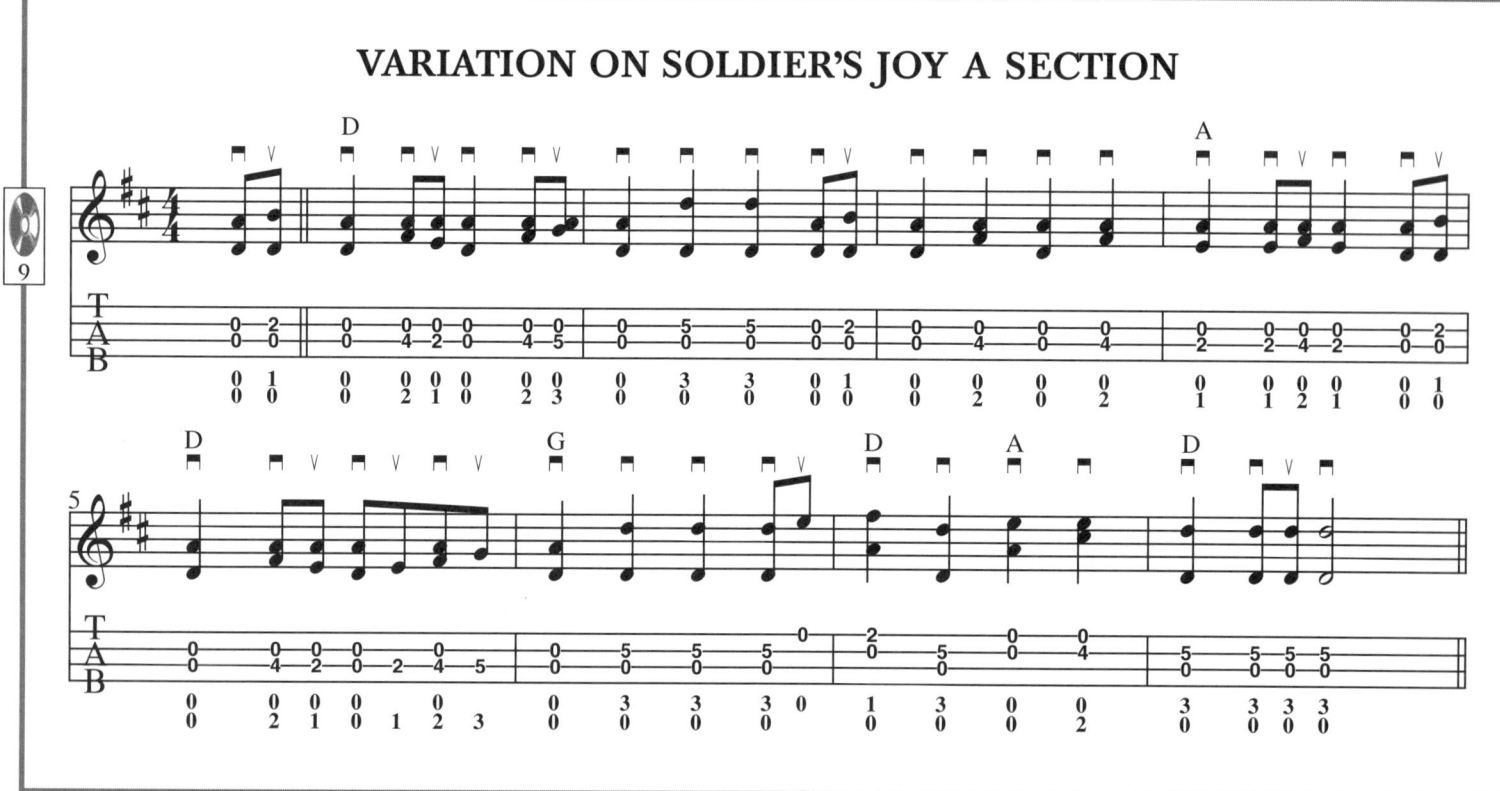

PLAYING IN THE KEY OF A

Here is the A Major scale in the first position of the mandolin. Note that the fingering on the first two strings is identical to that of the D Major scale (page 17) on the 2nd and 3rd strings.

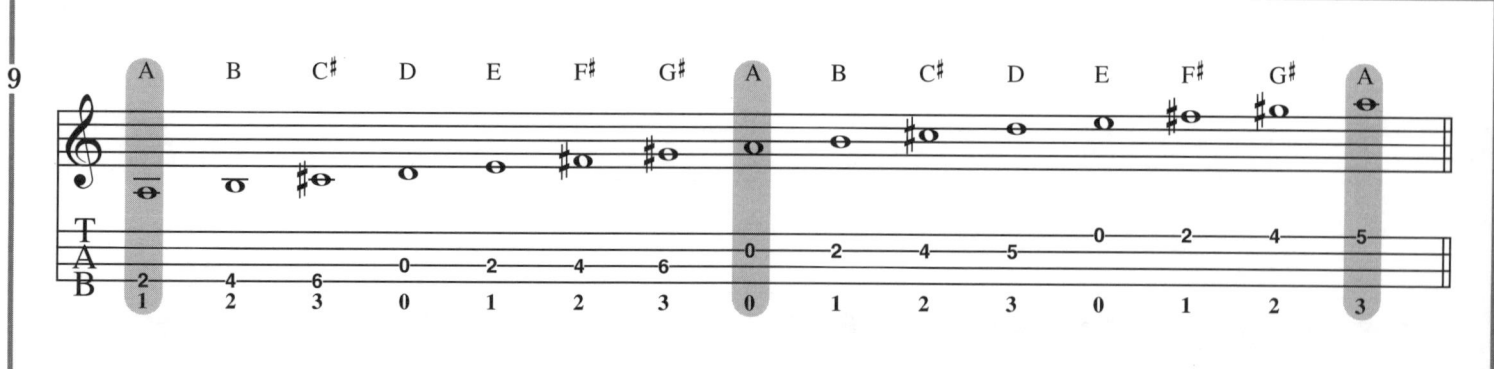

UNISON SLIDES

Another sound borrowed from the fiddle is the *unison slide*. A unison slide occurs when playing a melody note on an open string. To emphasize the melody note, slide up to the same note on the 7th fret of the adjacent lower string. For example, as you play the open-string melody note of the 1st-string E, strike the 2nd string simultaneously and slide up from the 5th to the 7th fret. This technique is used in the second half of "Old Joe Clark," along with some of the droning and harmony techniques you have already learned.

"Old Joe Clark" is another bluegrass, old-time standard. It has a bluesy sound due to the use of the *A Mixolydian mode*. A mode is just a reordering of a scale. The Mixolydian mode is a major scale beginning and ending on the 5th degree. Or, looking at it another way, the Mixolydian mode is a major scale with a 7th degree that has been lowered one half step (also called a ♭7), in this case, G-natural. This version incorporates unison slides, drone notes and harmony notes on adjacent strings.

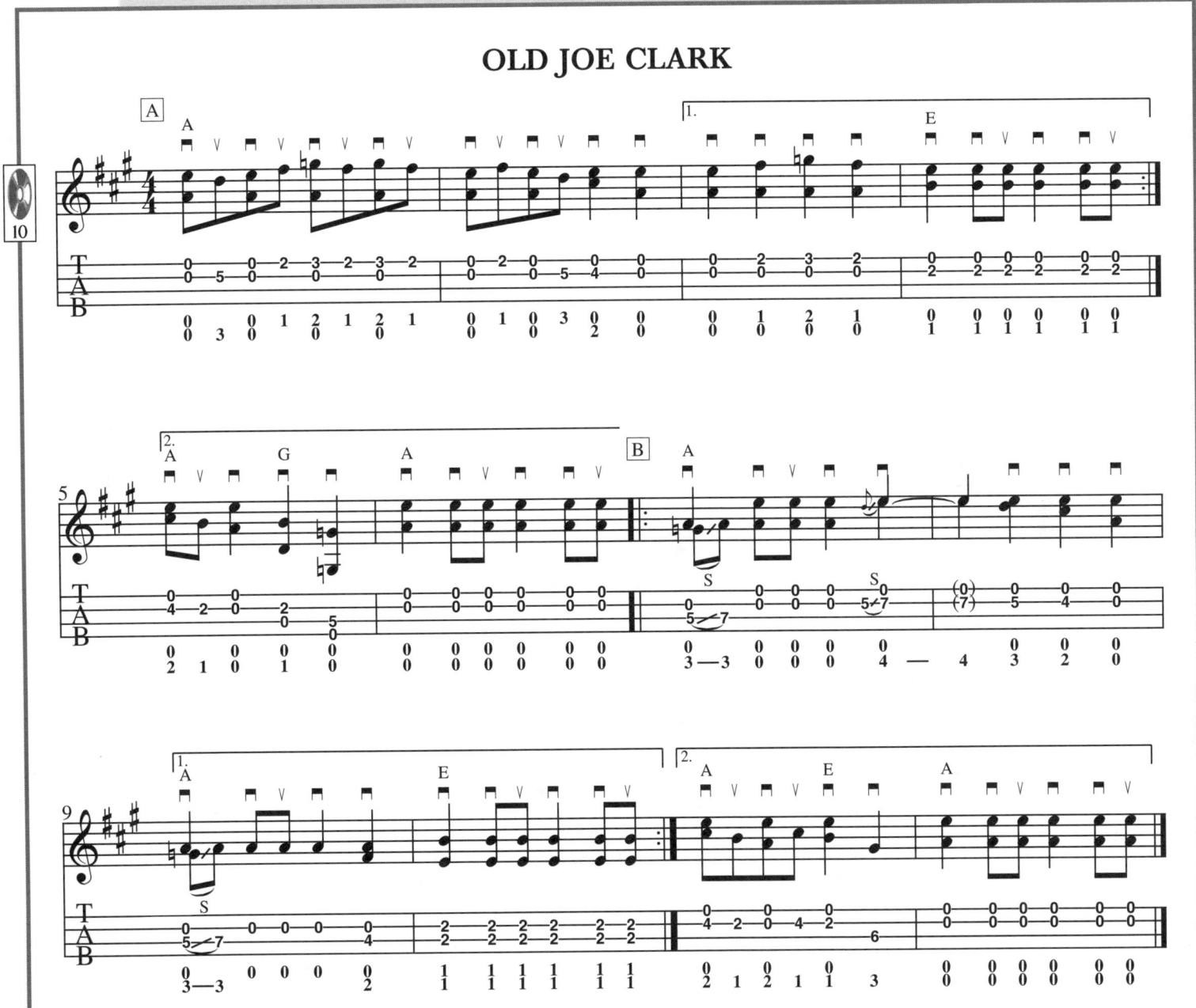

BLUES, MANDO-STYLE

The mandolin was an integral part of early black and white string bands in the 1920s and '30s. Two masters of the style were Howard "Louie Bluey" Armstrong (b. 1909) and Yank Rachell (1910–1997). Here is an eight-bar blues progression in the style of "Key to the Highway," which was written by Big Bill Broonzy and recorded by Eric Clapton (Derek and the Dominoes). Use the 7th-chord fingerings shown.

SWING 8THS
Notice that this tune is played in "swing 8ths," which means all the pairs of eighth notes are played unevenly, long-short, like an eighth-note triplet with the first two notes tied 🎵 = 🎵.

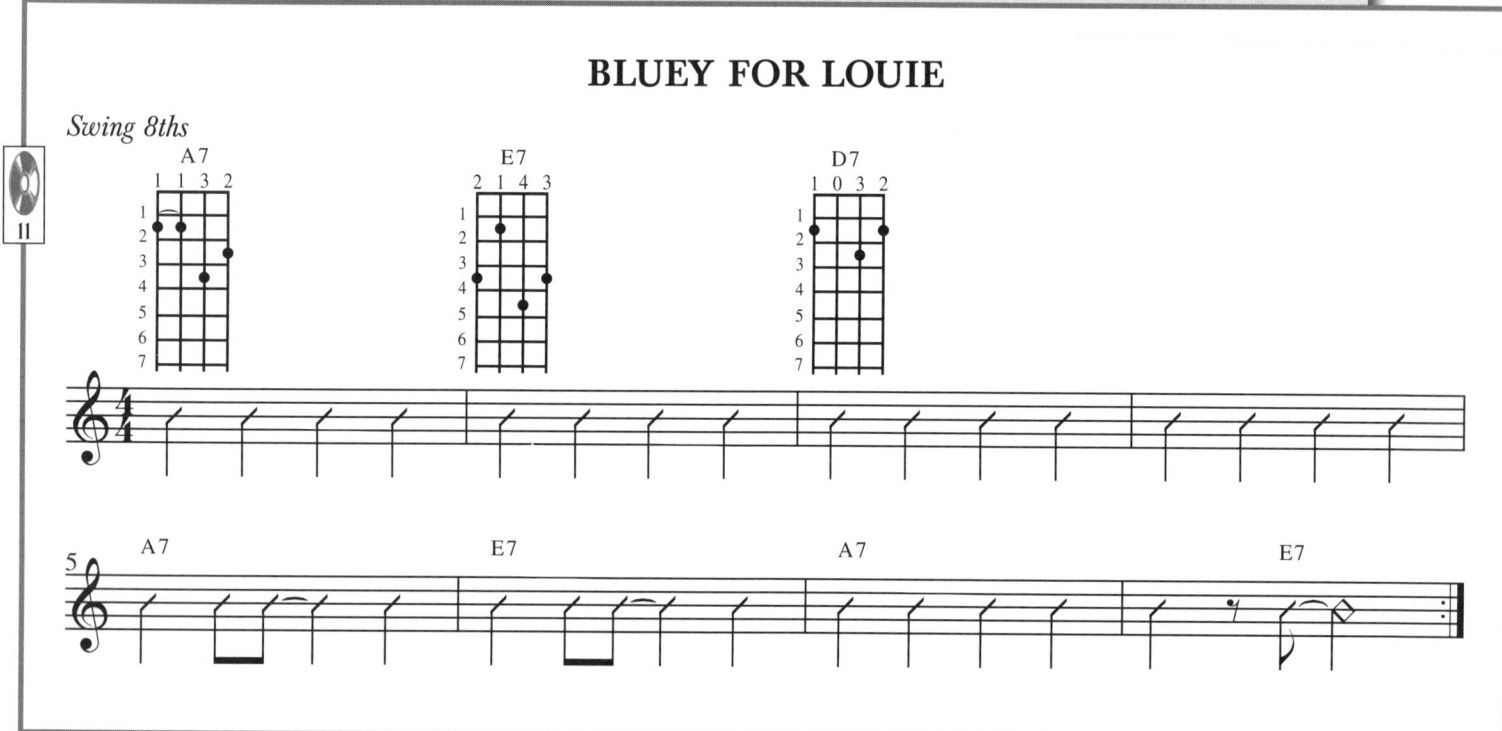

A BLUES SCALE FOR BLUES LEADS

Here is the *blues scale* for the key of A that mixes major and minor qualities. Notice that it uses both a ♭3rd and a major 3rd, plus it uses the infamous *blue note*, a ♭5. The notes and scale degrees are indicated. Pay special attention to the fingerings. We often use one finger to slide back and forth between two notes.

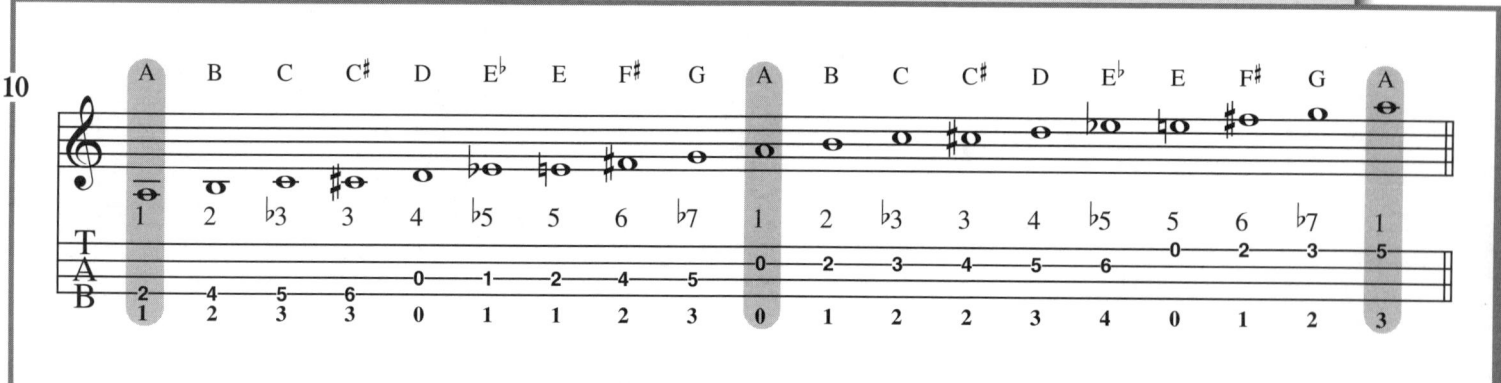

22 • The Multi-Instrumental Guitarist

Here is a sample blues solo for "Bluey for Louie." Watch for slides and harmony notes.

BLUEY FOR LOUIE SOLO

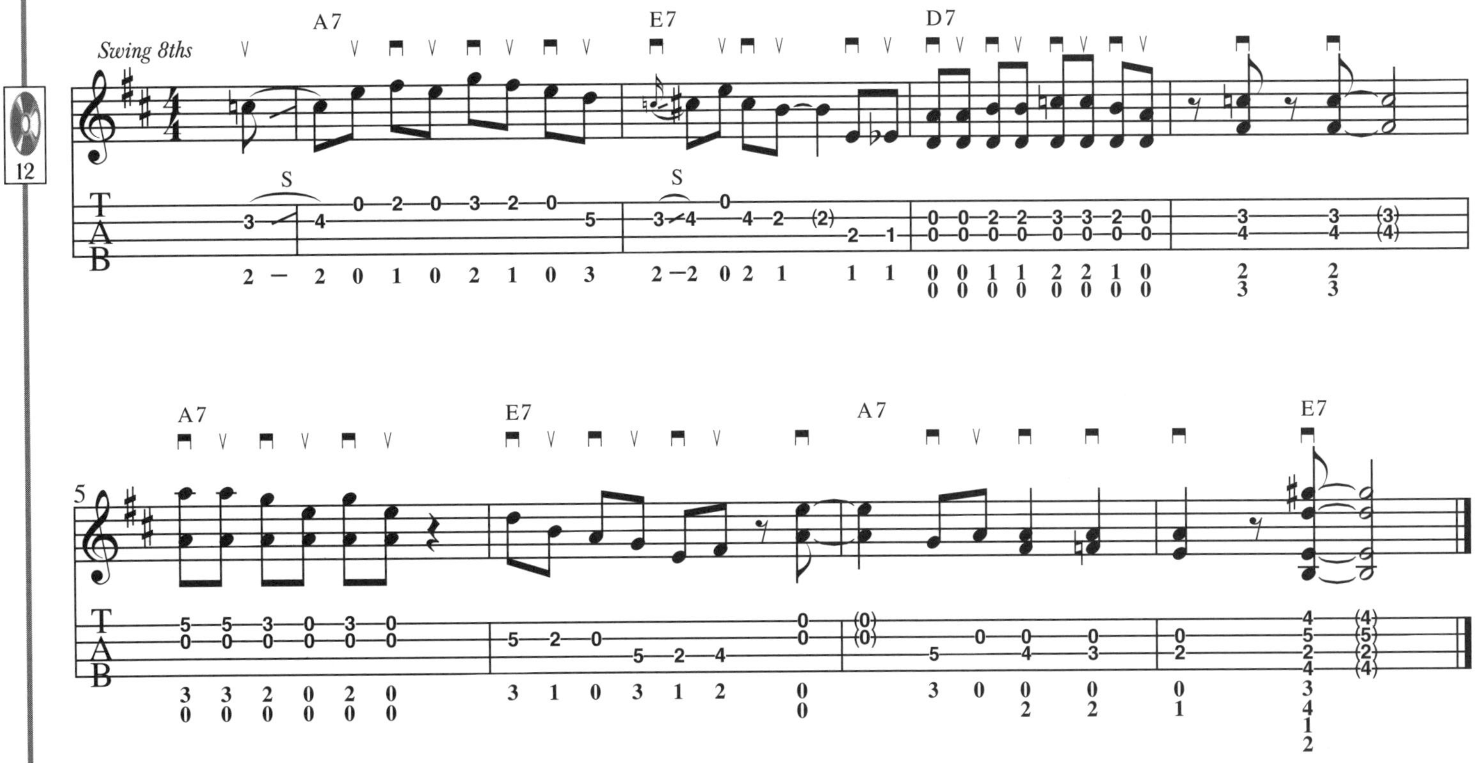

The longtime drummer and mandolinist for The Band, ***Levon Helm*** *(b. 1940), wore many musical hats throughout his long career, including multi-instrumentalist, songwriter, singer, impressario, studio owner, studio engineer and producer. The Band was among the first groups to incorporate traditional Appalachian instruments into the rock music of the 1960s and '70s.*

PHOTO BY DAVID SEELIG • COURTESY OF STAR FILEPHOTO,INC.

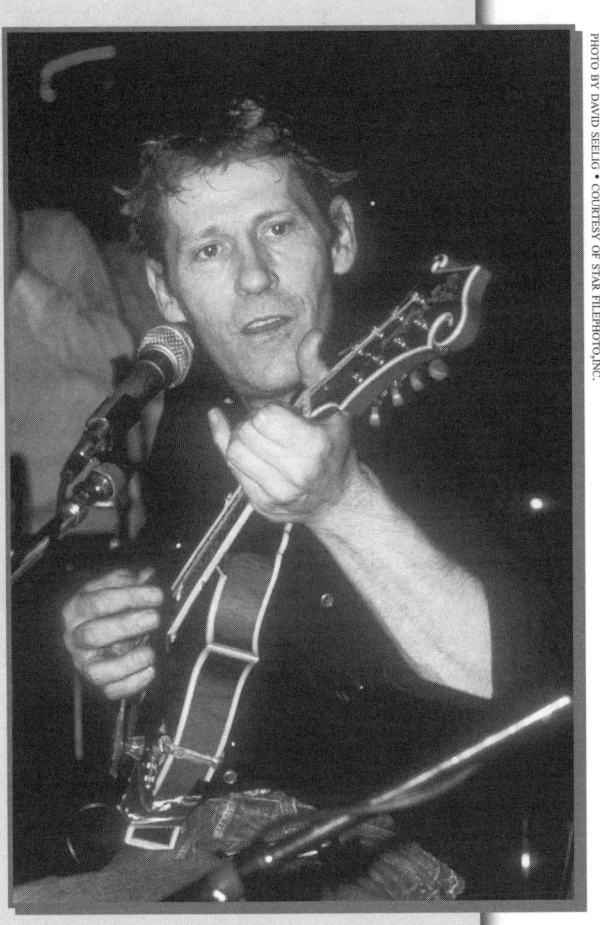

ROCK 'N' ROLL MANDOLIN

Since the early days of rock 'n' roll, the mandolin has been used to add new sounds to the standard guitar-bass-drum-keyboard combo. Jimmy Page used the mandolin to add a folksy jangle to Led Zeppelin's acoustic songs, while American artists such as The Band, R.E.M., Steve Earle, Wilco, and many others have incorporated the mandolin to expand the texture of their sound.

Rock mandolin builds on ideas from bluegrass, as well as folk and rock guitar. Often the mandolin is simply strummed using open chords (or chords in the higher positions). Here is a chord progression to try using a simple folk strum pattern.

THE BALLAD OF EXCELSIOR JONES

Another way to use the mandolin in a rock context is to incorporate *arpeggios* (broken chords) and small melodic figures into the chord progression. Here is the chord progression of "The Ballad of Excelsior Jones" with some arpeggios and melodic passing tones added to connect the chords.

THE IMPROVED BALLAD OF EXCELSIOR JONES

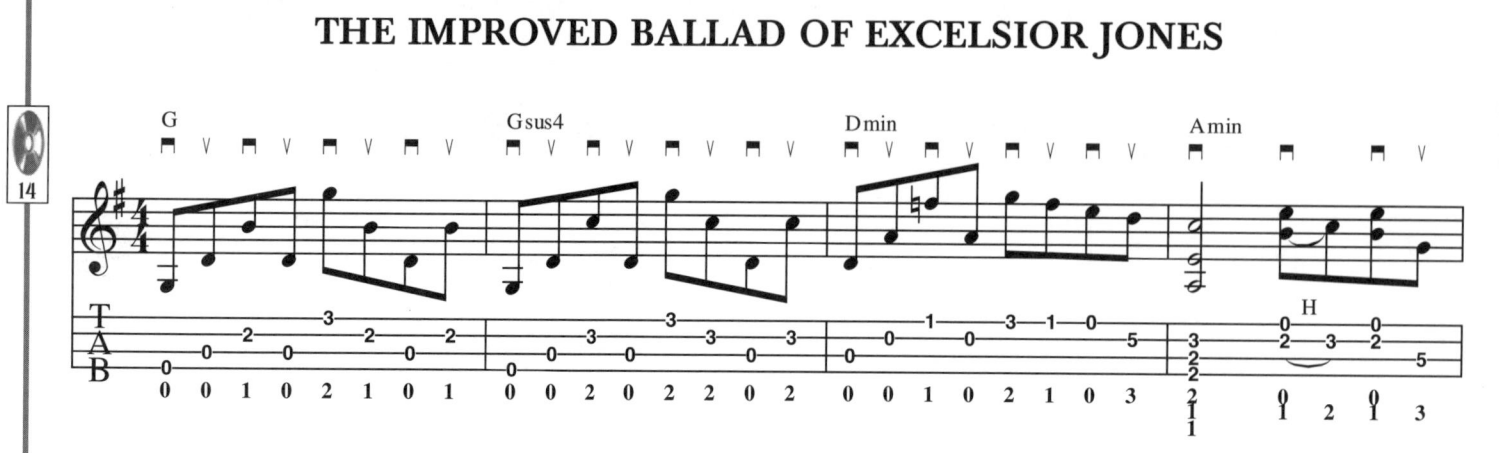

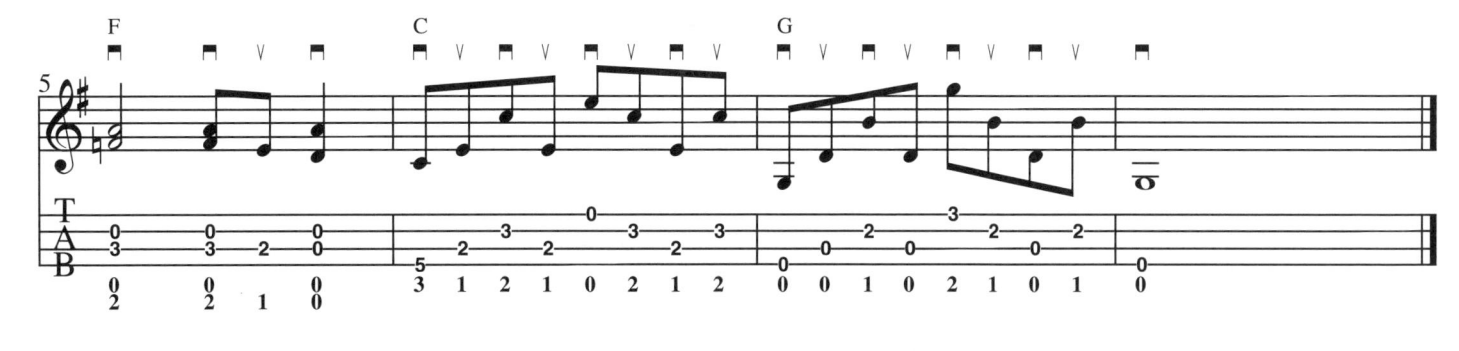

Now try this solo using a G Mixolydian mode. In the key of G, this means that the F# of the G Major scale has been changed to F♮. Chord symbols are provided to give you a harmonic context for the solo; you will not hear a chord part on the CD.

THE SOLO ON THE IMPROVED BALLAD OF EXCELSIOR JONES

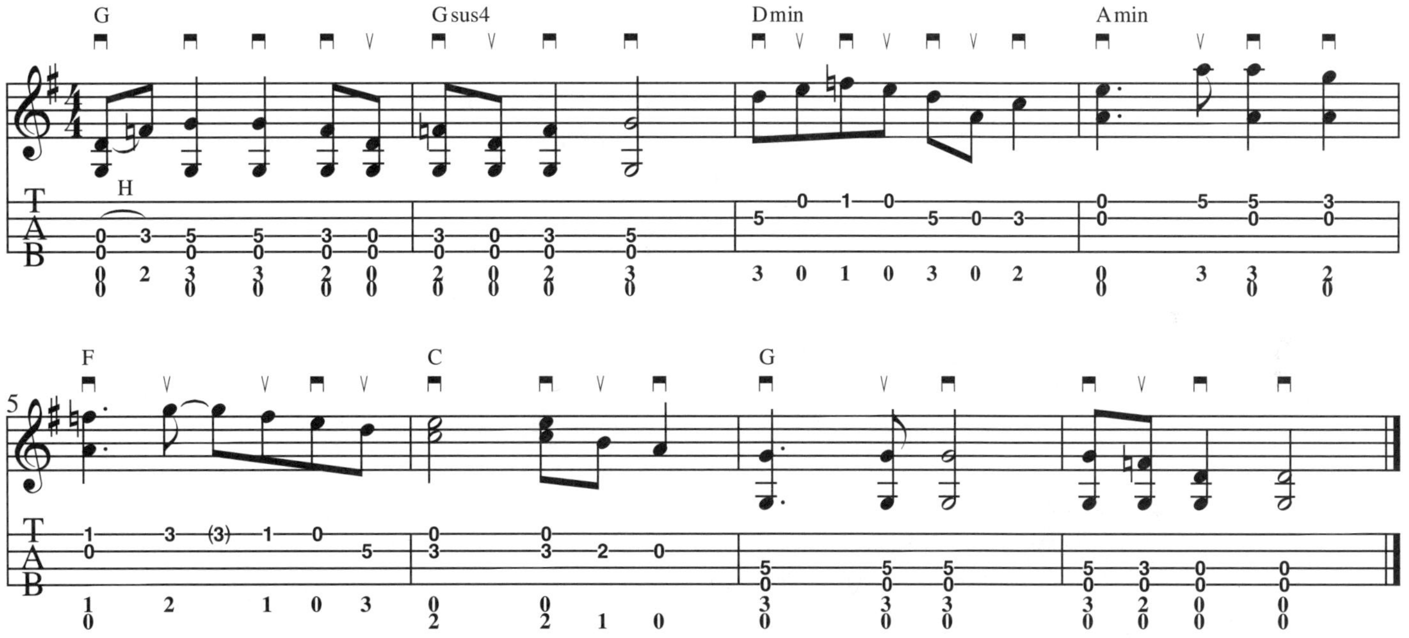

CHAPTER 2
THE "OCTAVE MANDOLIN" GROUP: OCTAVE MANDOLIN, IRISH BOUZOUKI, IRISH TENOR BANJO

In the 1960s and '70s, folk music of the British Isles went through a renaissance similar to the American folk revival happening at the time. New instruments and influences were added as musicians developed the driving, propulsive sound of modern Celtic folk music. Several instruments used in the Celtic sound share the same tuning and very similar playing techniques.

THE IRISH BOUZOUKI
The Irish *bouzouki* developed through the playing of Andy Irvine and Donal Lunny, who used imported traditional Greek bouzoukis and tuned them to fit Irish music. Structural changes were also made. The Irish bouzouki (sometimes called a *cittern*) is a flat-topped, teardrop-shaped instrument with a flat or slightly arched back. The neck is similar to a guitar neck, but often slightly shorter. Like a mandolin, the bouzouki has eight strings arranged in four courses (sets of strings). It is tuned an octave below the mandolin. Some bouzoukis use octave double strings on the lowest two courses, similar to the 12-string guitar. Whether you use octave double strings or unison double strings is a matter of preference. There are also some tuning variations, but in this book we will use unison double strings (in the octave mandolin tuning).

THE OCTAVE MANDOLIN
The *octave mandolin* is very similar to the Irish bouzouki. It generally has a shorter neck and uses only unison double strings. Some have an arched top. It is tuned an octave below the mandolin, hence the name.

THE IRISH TENOR BANJO
The Irish *tenor banjo* goes farther back in the tradition than the bouzouki. It dates to the 1920s and '30s, when tenor banjos were popular parlor and big-band instruments in America and Europe. Modern players have adopted the octave mandolin tuning on this instrument for Celtic music, instead of the traditional tenor banjo tuning of C–G–D–A (see pages 34–37). The tenor banjo has only four strings. You could also tune a four-string *tenor guitar* to this tuning.

While there are nuances that are unique to the playing of each instrument, the music and techniques in this chapter can be easily applied to any of the instruments shown on page 26. The octave mandolin sound has a depth and openness that sets it apart from six-string guitar. You don't have to search out an expensive instrument to give it a try. Just keep your eyes out for anything with four courses (or single strings) and a scale length (nut to bridge) of around 19 to 24 inches. Steel strings will work best, and you may need to experiment with gauges.

OCTAVE MANDOLIN TUNING

Below is the octave mandolin tuning. If you have a bouzouki with octave doubles on the 3rd and 4th courses, just tune them an octave higher than their mates. For an illustration of the notes on the neck, see page 10, in the mandolin chapter. Note that the music for the mandolin and octave mandolin looks identical. Like the guitar, the octave mandolin sounds one octave lower than written.

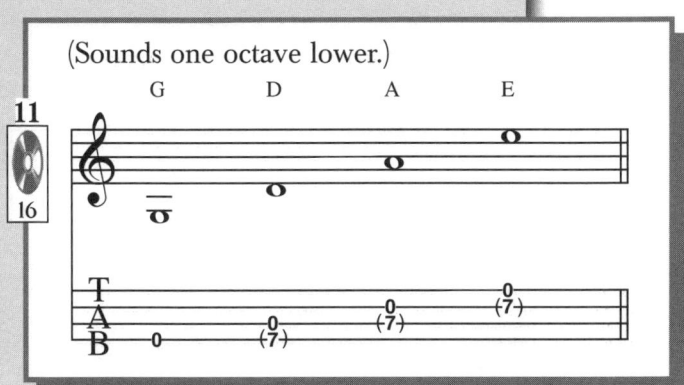

CHORDS

Here are some open chord shapes to try. Note that these are the same as the mandolin, but some of the fingerings have changed to accommodate the longer scale length.

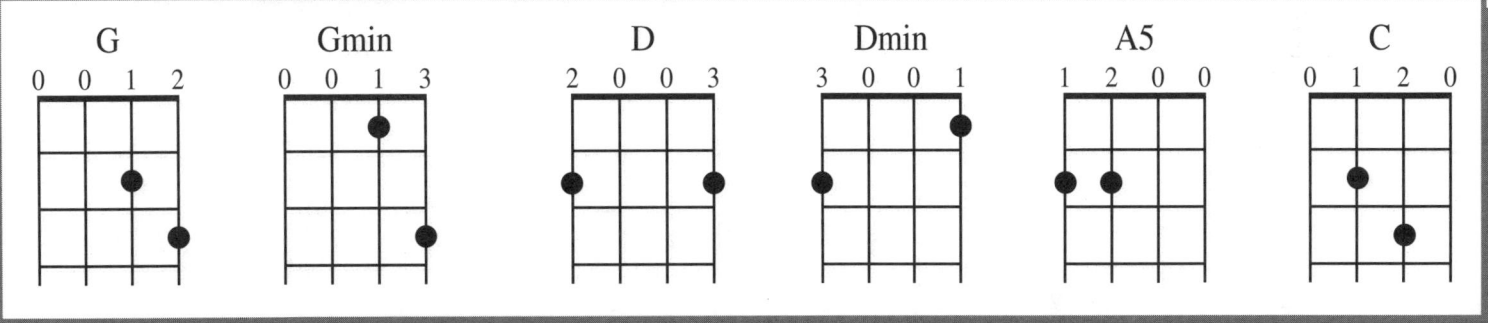

MOVABLE CHORD SHAPES

The strings that have the roots of these chords have been marked with an "R." You can play any one of these chords on any root by simply moving to the desired root on the marked string(s).

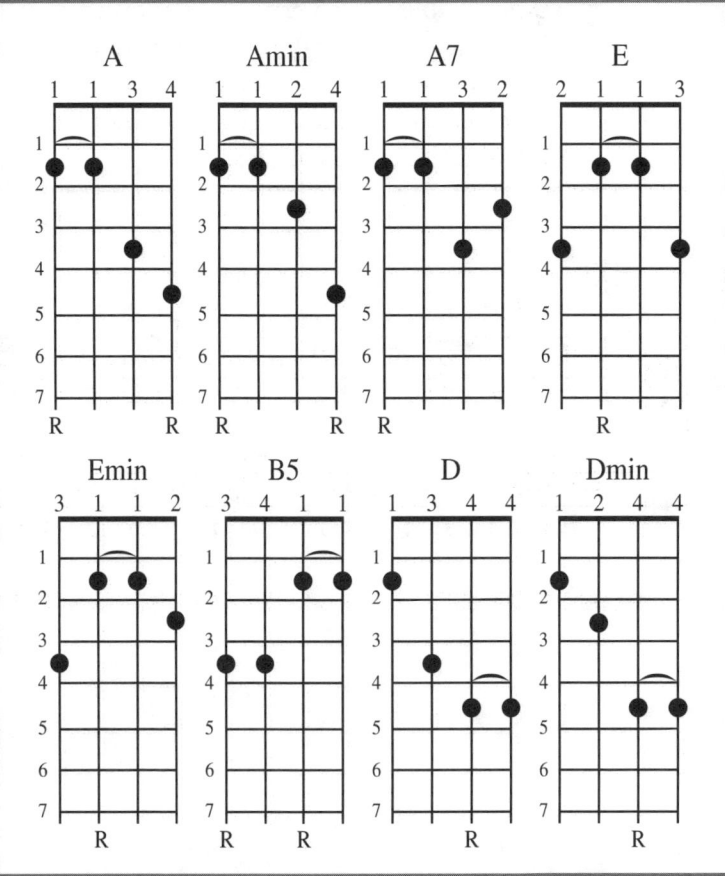

The Multi-Instrumental Guitarist • 27

MULTI-INSTRUMENTAL MAYHEM:
While this chapter is designed to accommodate the special fingerings and scale length of the octave mandolin instruments, you may also want to try the material in the mandolin chapter with these instruments. Some of the chord fingerings may not work, and the melody fingerings will need adjustment, but the tablature and the music will work fine! Likewise, try some of the music in this chapter on a mandolin (just be sure to adjust the fingerings).

Below is the E Dorian mode. The minor sound of the Dorian mode is common in Celtic and Appalachian music. The E Dorian mode is like E Major with lowered third and seventh degrees (♭3 and ♭7). Dorian is the second mode of the major scale, so E Dorian has the same notes as the D Major scale (E is the second degree of a D scale). Play the D Major scale starting and ending on E, and you've got E Dorian. For the more common G, D and A Major scales, check pages 16–20 of the mandolin chapter.

E DORIAN MODE

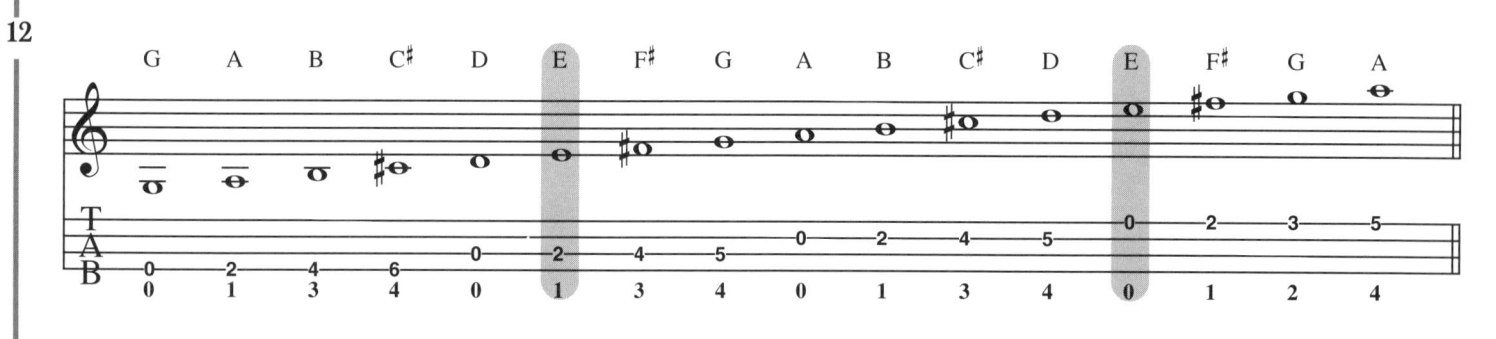

IRISH ORNAMENTS

Irish music has many *ornaments* or decorative techniques that are drawn from fiddle and bagpipe playing. Two very common ornaments are *triplets* and *turns*. These are especially popular in the playing of the octave mandolin instruments, particularly the tenor banjo. The triplet is simply a rhythmic variation in which the beat is divided into three equal parts. A turn involves adding a rapid group of notes that surround (moving just above and below) the main pitch. Try these examples.

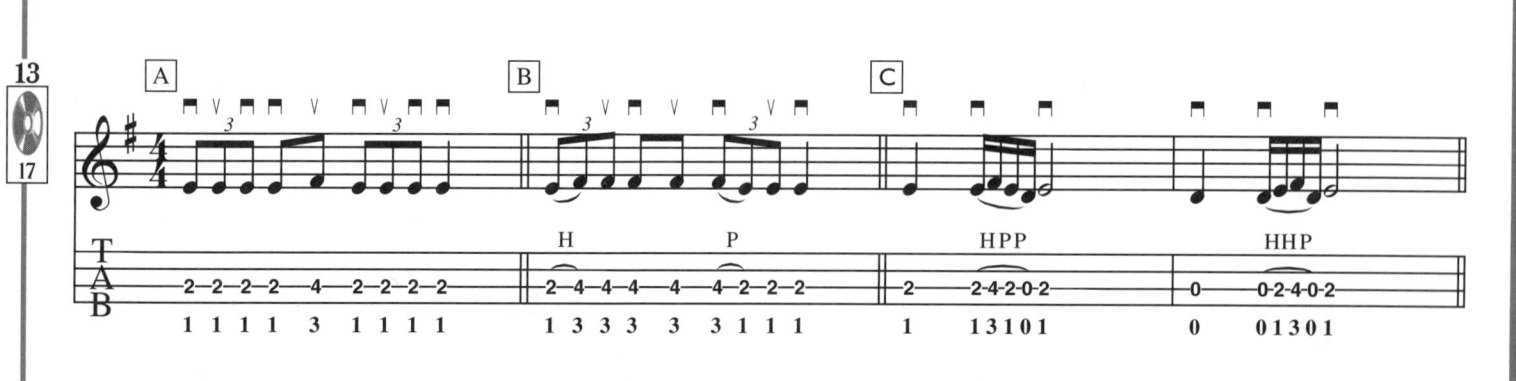

This is a common tune heard in Celtic and even Appalachian jam sessions. It is particularly well suited to the octave mandolin instruments. "Drowsy Maggie" uses the E Dorian mode.

DROWSY MAGGIE

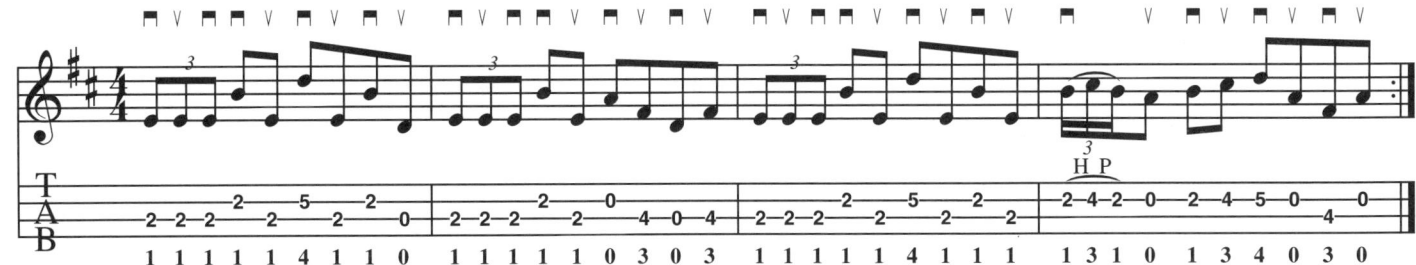

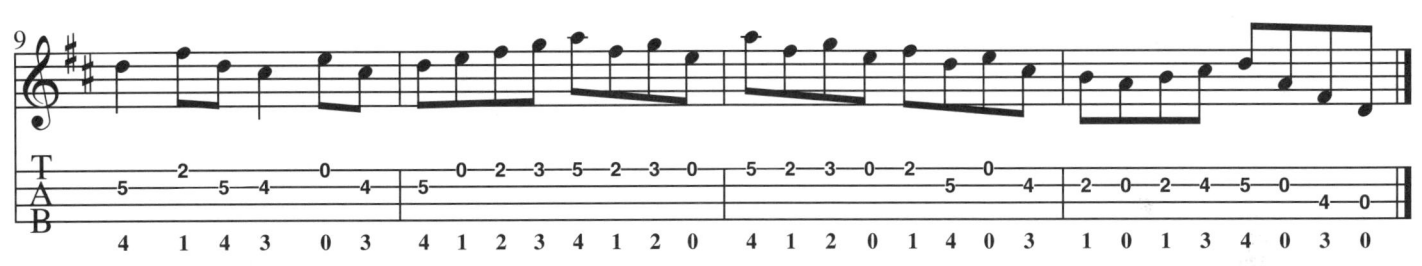

Tim O'Brien is one of Nashville's most respected multi-instrumentalists. A gifted singer and songwriter, O'Brien is also extremely accomplished on guitar, mandolin and bazouki. He can be heard on solo albums, in duets with his sister Mollie, and as a leader of Hot Rize.

PLAYING JIGS

The Irish bouzouki in particular has risen up as a popular rhythm instrument for jigs (quick dances in 6/8 time). It provides the chord work of the guitar with the rhythmic drive of the *Bodhran*, the traditional Irish frame drum. Below are some strum patterns to get you in the 6/8 groove. Notice that in 6/8, there are two three-part beats per measure. The dotted quarter note gets one beat.

JIG RHYTHM PATTERN NO.1
This pattern is a simple, sparse rhythm favored by banjo players for a more traditional sound. It is very similar to the "boom-chick" rhythm heard in bluegrass. Try it with many chords.

JIG RHYTHM PATTERN NO.2
This pattern involves strumming all the strings, so no TAB is needed. Notice the accent marks (>). Without these accents, it is very hard to hear the two-beat pulse of the 6/8 rhythm. This pattern is great for bouzoukis and octave mandolins, but it can be a bit aggressive on the banjo.

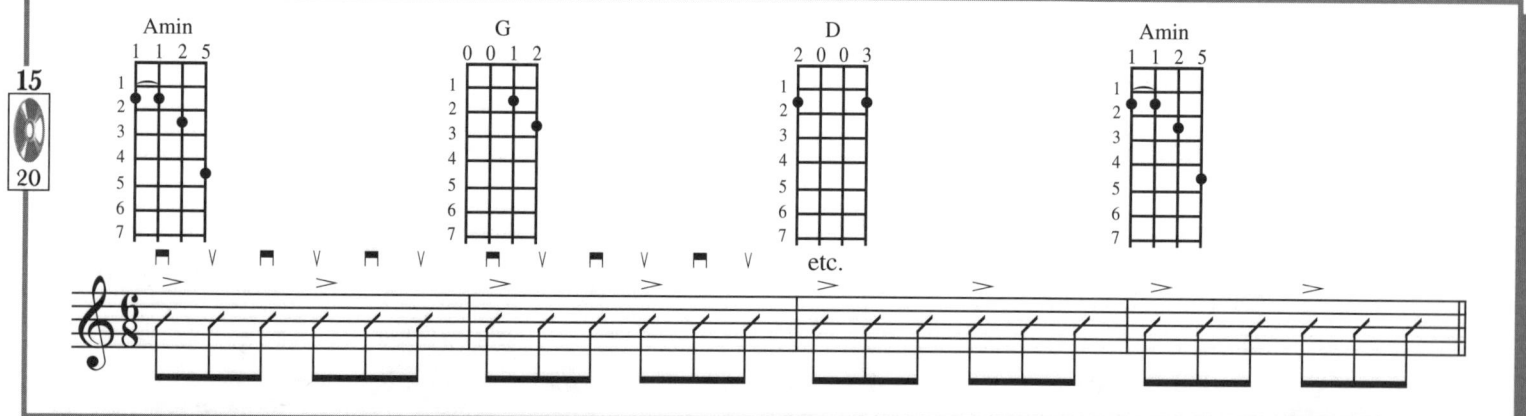

JIG RHYTHM PATTERN NO.3
This is a variation on Jig Rhythm Pattern No.2. It creates a syncopated accent pattern; the accents are shifted from the first part of each beat to the second and third parts. By interchanging Patterns No.2 and No.3, and adding your own variations, you can imitate the drive and pulse of the Bodhran drum. Use the chord fingerings indicated in Pattern No.2.

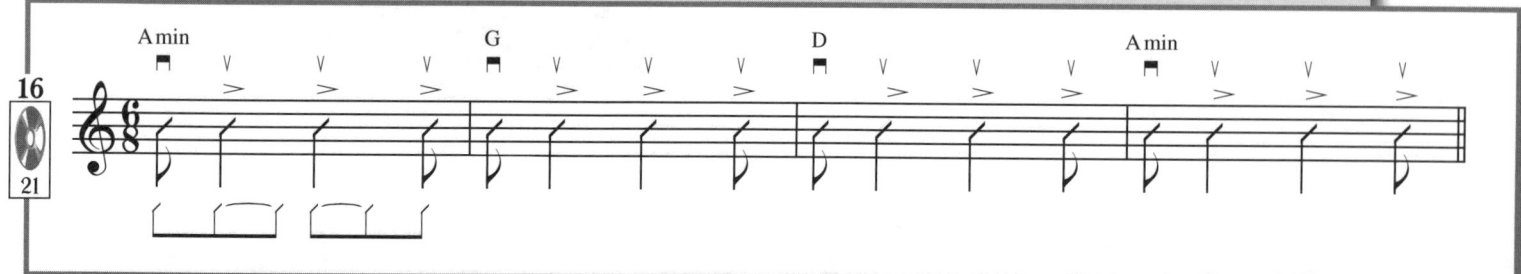

30 • The Multi-Instrumental Guitarist

Try this traditional jam session favorite using a mixture of Jig Rhythm Patterns #2 and #3. Try to exaggerate the accents at first, so you can develop a natural feel for the $\frac{6}{8}$ groove. Use the chord fingerings indicated on the previous page. Be sure to learn the melody that follows on page 33.

SCATTER THE MUD (CHORDS AND RHYTHM)

Here is the A Dorian mode, which is derived from the G Major scale (played starting and ending on A).

THE A DORIAN MODE

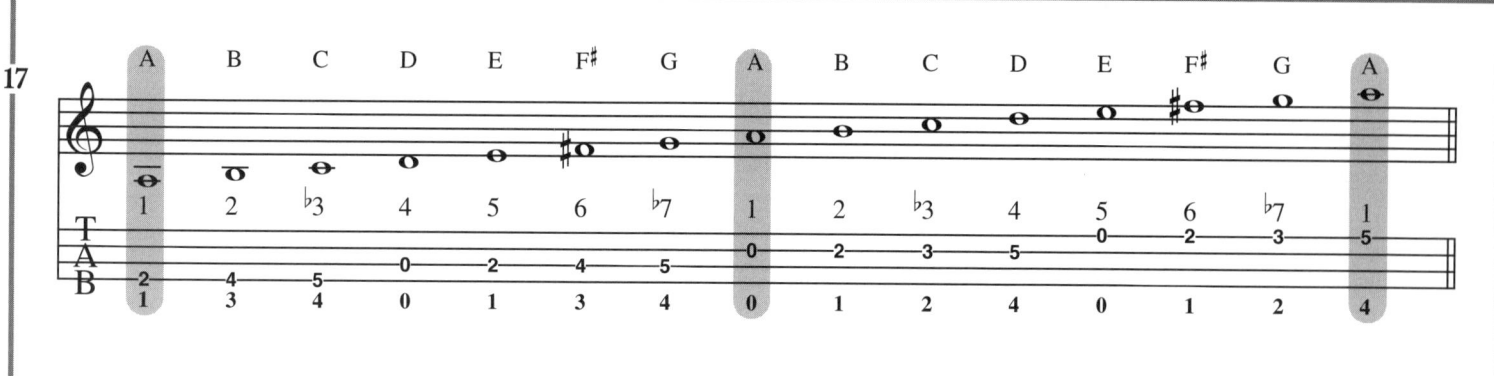

JIG MELODIES

Jig melodies can be a bit tricky. The notes are arranged in two groups of three in each measure. You will generally start the first group with a downstroke. Therefore, the second group must start with an upstroke. Using strong accents at first will help you feel the beat. Playing the rhythm patterns on pages 30–31 will also help. Try these examples and exaggerate the accents!

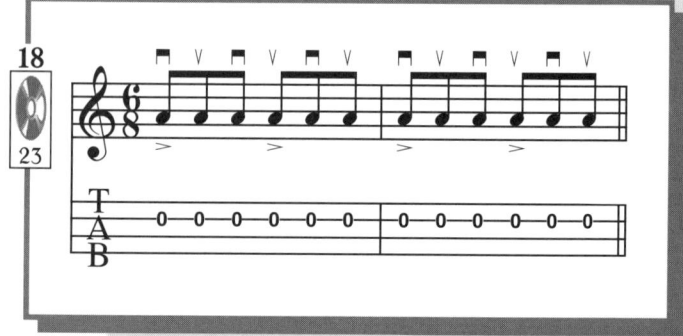

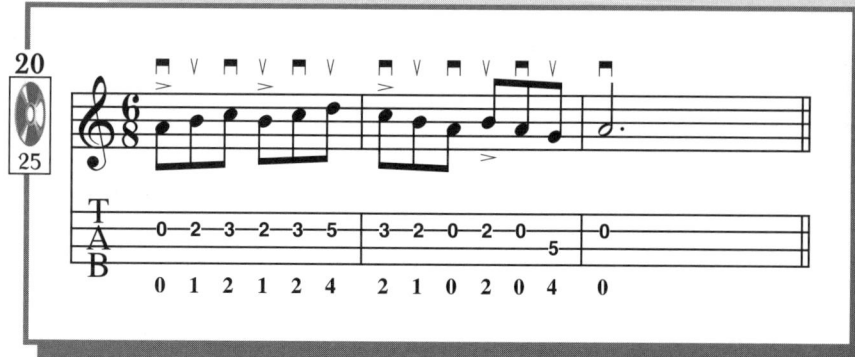

32 • The Multi-Instrumental Guitarist

Here is the melody for "Scatter the Mud" (you learned the rhythm part on page 31). Take it slowly, one line at a time. Make sure to follow the fingerings and pickings indicated. Also, expect some sixteenth-note ornaments.

SCATTER THE MUD (MELODY)

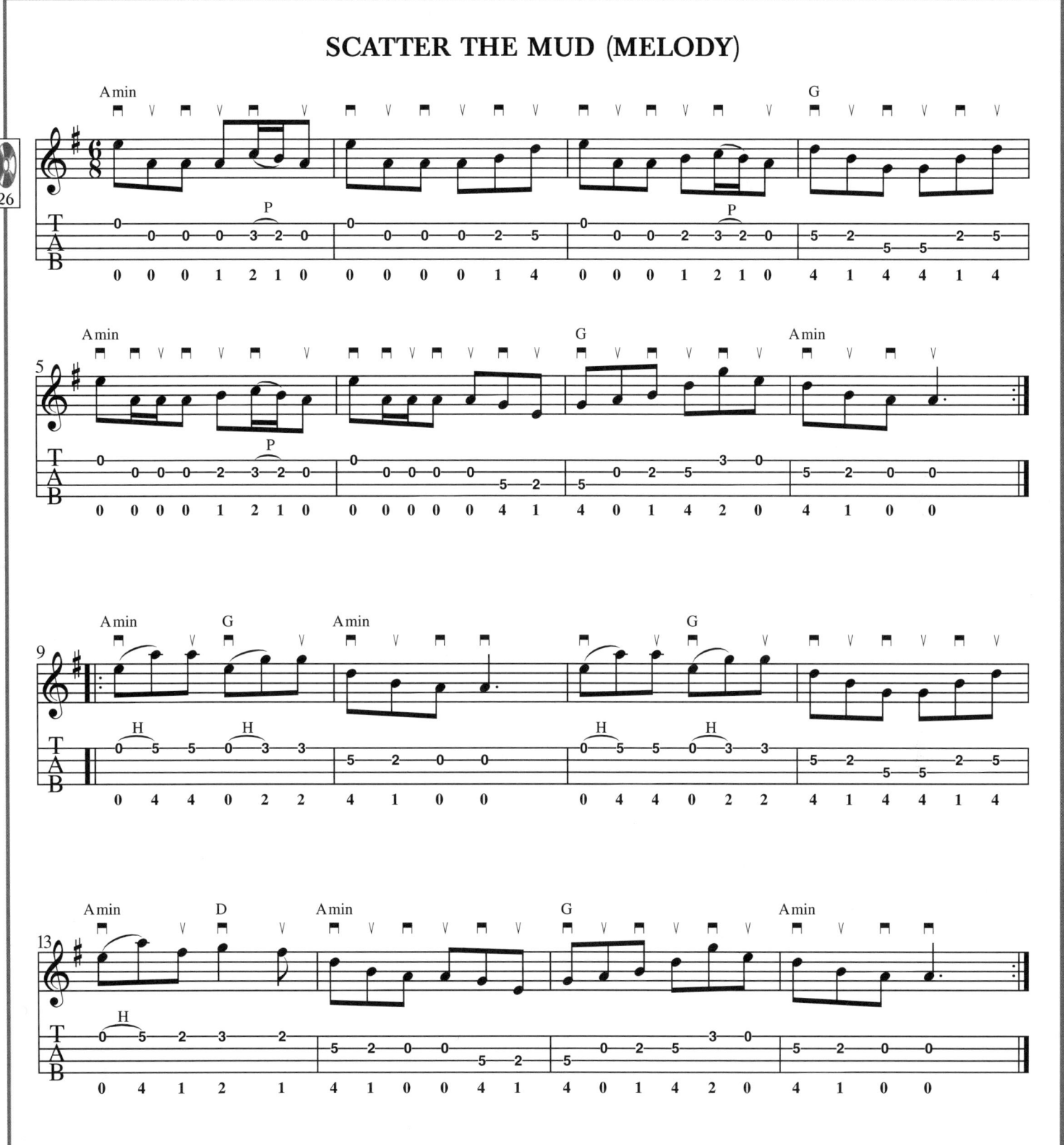

CHAPTER 3
TENOR BANJO AND TENOR GUITAR SWING AND DIXIELAND

These instruments are closely related to the octave mandolin group discussed in Chapter 2 in that they are also tuned in 5ths. *Tenor banjo* and *tenor guitar*, both four-string instruments which were popular in the jazz age of the 1920s and '30s, are still relatively easy to find today.

Tenor Guitar

Tenor Banjo

TENOR GUITAR TUNING

As you learned in Chapter 2, most four-string banjos used for Irish music are tuned an octave below the mandolin. Many players also use this tuning for tenor guitars. (If you choose to tune these instruments to this tuning, use the tunings and fingerings found in Chapter 2.) Another popular choice is to tune the tenor banjo or tenor guitar to the first four strings of a guitar (see Chapter 6). In this chapter, we will use the tuning most common to the jazz-age performers on four-string instruments, which is identical to that of the viola: one 5th below the violin or mandolin. Here are the open strings and matching frets.

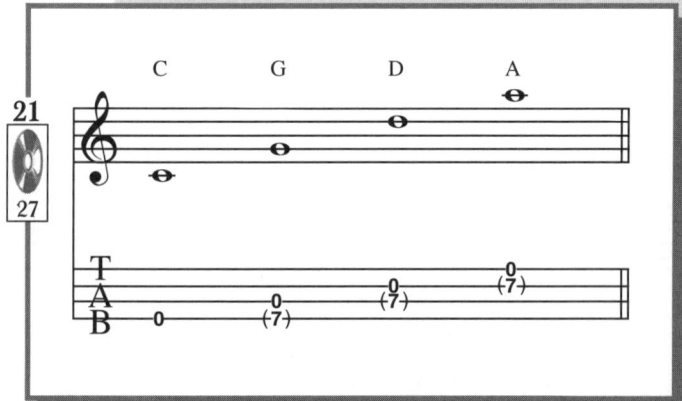

> *MULTI-INSTRUMENTAL MADNESS*
> The C–G–D–A tuning is also the tuning for the *mandola*, a fairly rare cousin of the mandolin. The even less common *mandocello* is also tuned this way but one octave lower. These instruments were popular in mandolin orchestras in the 1920s. Mandolas and mandocellos still show up in old-time and Celtic jam sessions. They are played just like octave mandolins, but they require you to transpose your scales and chord forms to fit the new tuning. If you are lucky enough to have a mandola or mandocello, the chords and examples in this chapter should help.

34 • The Multi-Instrumental Guitarist

OPEN CHORDS

These shapes are identical to those used by mandolin and octave mandolin, but you must transpose down a 5th. So, the first chord form is what you used for a G chord on the mandolin, but now it sounds like a C chord.

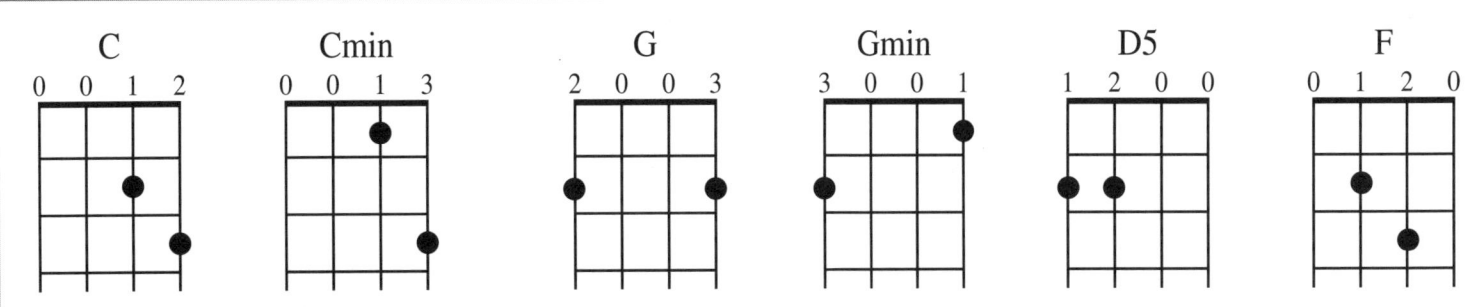

MOVABLE CHORDS

Here are some movable chord shapes for tenor instruments. The chord tones (root, 3rd, 5th, 7th) are indicated to help you move the chords around on the neck. The chords are arranged in rows and columns so you can see the major, minor and 7th versions of each shape. Note that there is a new shape (the third column of chords) that did not appear in the octave mandolin chapter. This shape is easy to play on the short scale of the four-string instruments, but is a bit unwieldy on the eight-string instruments (such as the mandolin).

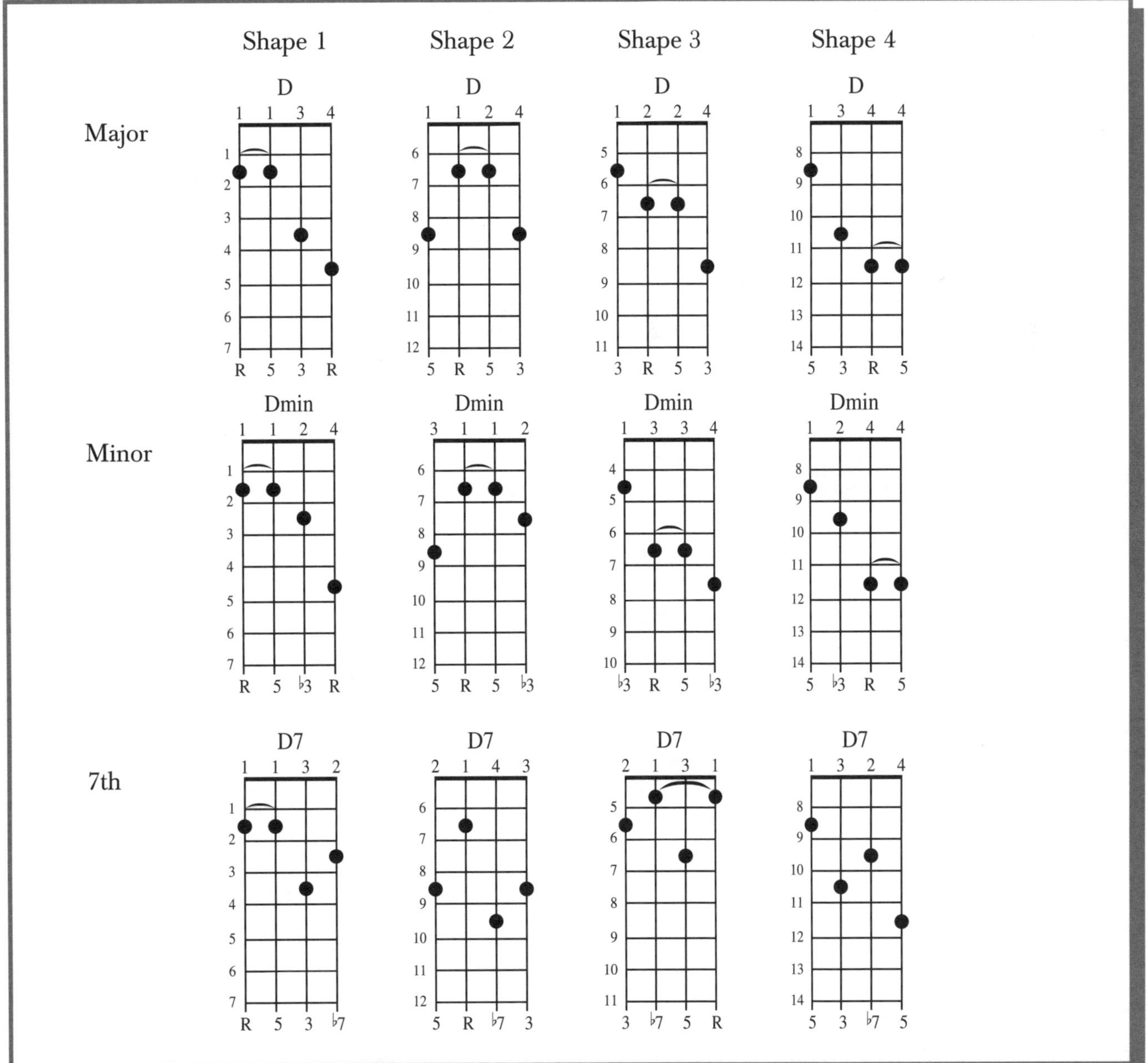

MULTI-INSTRUMENTAL MADNESS

For more practice on your tenor instrument, try the examples in Chapter 1 (mandolin) and Chapter 2 (octave mandolin). Use the same frets and strings. You may want to adjust fingerings. The keys will be different on the tenor instruments, since it is transposed down a 5th from a mandolin, but the tunes will provide some useful practice material.

LEAD TENOR BANJO/GUITAR

Soloing in the early swing style involves a mixture of scales and chords. The horn-like, single-note jazz-guitar style blossomed with the electric six-string guitar. Below is a *C Blues* scale for the tenor instruments. This particular scale is based on a major scale with the addition of lowered 3rds and 7ths (♭3 and ♭7). The fingering of this scale is organized in three octaves, starting in open position. Notice that as you move up the neck in the second and third octaves, the fingering pattern remains the same.

C BLUES SCALE

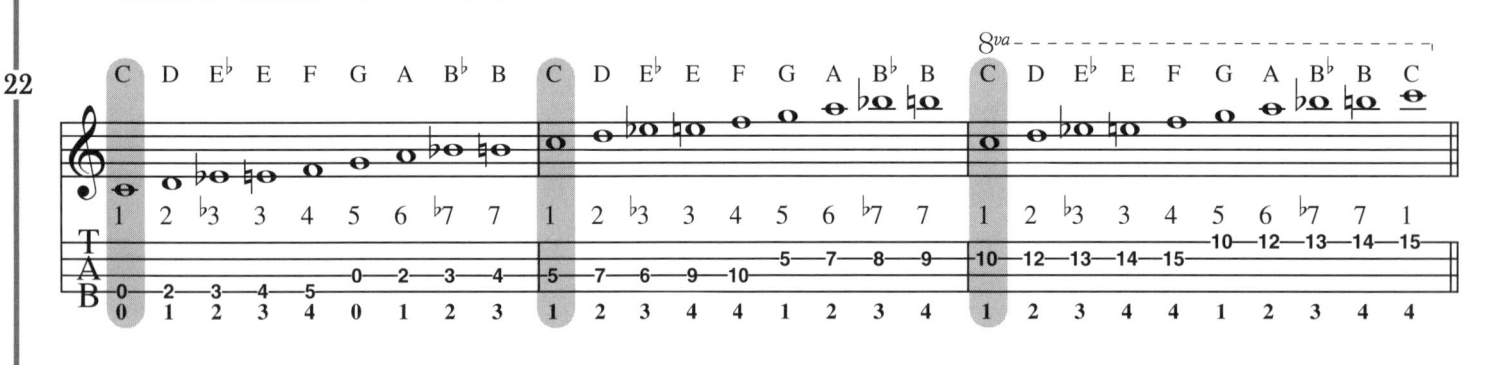

DIXIELAND RHYTHM STYLE

The most recognized sound of the tenor banjo and guitar is the rhythmic chord style used in Dixieland and swing music of the 1920s and '30s. Players used chord inversions to traverse the entire range of the fingerboard. Strumming was loud and percussive to cut through the band in the pre-amplified age, and involved a strong rhythmic pulse. Syncopation is used to create a jazz feel.

Following is a version of "When the Saints Go Marching In" using the chord shapes and scale you have just learned. Watch out for the syncopated strumming.

CHAPTER 4
INTRODUCING THE FIVE-STRING BANJO

THE HAPPIEST INSTRUMENT KNOWN TO HUMANITY

Speaking through the Peanuts character Linus, Charles Schultz once wrote that in order to improve the state of the world and the human condition, every newborn child should be issued a banjo. Of course, he never said anything about the soundproofed rooms in which the conscientious banjoists should practice.

The five-string banjo is a staple of bluegrass and old-time music, and the raucous-sounding five-string banjoist is the butt of all the best jokes. Here are the basic pieces and parts of the five-string banjo.

THE PARTS OF THE BANJO

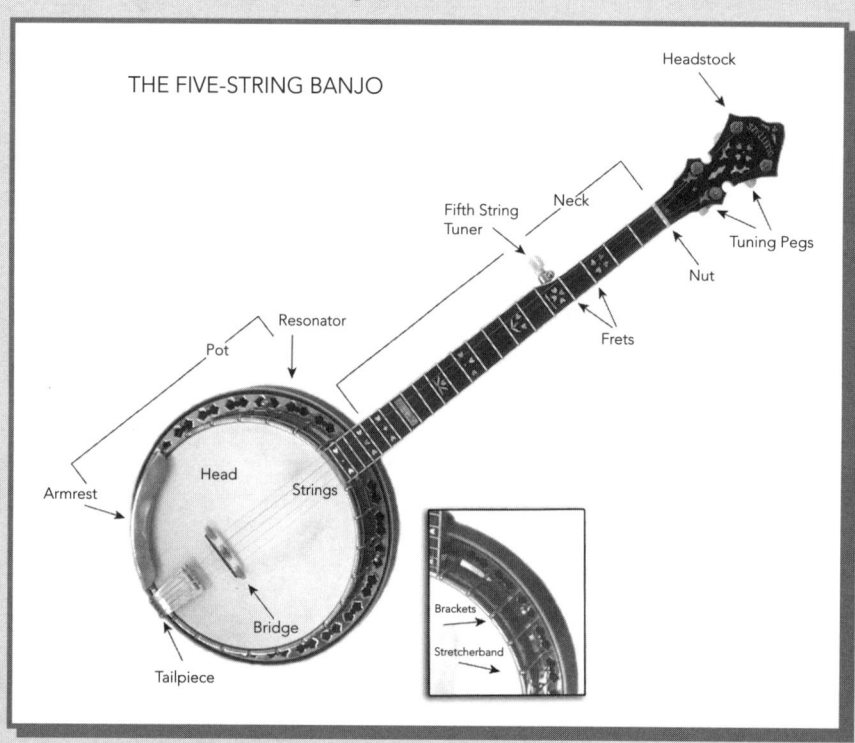

VARIATIONS IN CONSTRUCTION

There are a few variations on the standard (five-string) banjo. Some banjos do not have a *resonator* (the solid wood back of the body). These are called open-back banjos and are preferred by old-time *clawhammer* (see page 41) players for their "plunkier" sound. They are also not as piercingly loud as the resonator banjo.

There are many varieties in the *head* material, from clear or frosted plastic to animal hide (rare, but still used) and "Fiberskyn," a synthetic material made by Remo, the drum and percussion company, to approximate the look and sound of animal hide.

Some banjos are made with a brass *tone ring* on which the head rests just inside the rim. These banjos are heavier and more expensive, but generally have a louder, more bell-like tone.

WHAT TO LOOK FOR

Make sure you get a banjo with a five-string neck. Four-string necks are used for *plectrum* (pick), or "tenor" playing common in Irish and swing music (see Chapter 3). Make sure there are no rips in the head, no loose brackets and a comfortable *action* (distance from strings to fingerboard). Finally, make sure the *tuners* work well. Bad tuners will drive you crazy later!

SOME HANDY DEVICES

You will want to get a *capo* (a device placed around the fingerboard to raise the pitch of the strings) to allow you to play in different keys in higher positions up the neck of the banjo. You can either use a guitar capo, or a shorter one designed specifically for banjo. The capo only affects the first four strings. You will need another device to raise the pitch of the 5th string to match your tuning when using a capo. Some players simply tune the 5th string up higher. This works for traditional clawhammer playing, but can interfere with some runs that use fretted notes on the 5th string.

Some banjoists have *spikes* installed between the frets on the 5th string. These are actually tiny model railroad spikes that can be found at hobby stores. When these have been properly installed (by an experienced professional) you can hook the 5th string under the spike to raise its pitch.

Another option is the *5th string capo*. There are a variety of these contraptions available, most of which consist of a screw mechanism on a sliding rail attached to the neck. These work well but can get in the way of your left hand thumb as you go up the neck, and are more conspicuous than spikes.

5-STRING BANJO TUNING

Many tunings are used for the banjo. The most common tuning for bluegrass banjo (also common for old-time banjo) is G tuning. This tuning is very closely related to open G tuning on the guitar (the first four strings are identical). If you are familiar with open G on the guitar, you will be able to transfer chord shapes and scales you have learned on the first four strings. Below are the notes and matching frets on adjacent strings for G tuning on the banjo. Like the guitar, the notes on the banjo sound an octave lower than written.

OPEN G TUNING

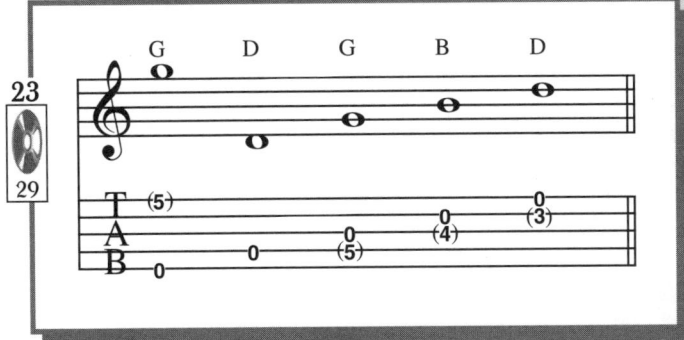

NOTES ON THE BANJO IN G TUNING

Below are the notes on the banjo fingerboard. Note that the 5th string notes are identical to those of the 1st string above the 5th fret.

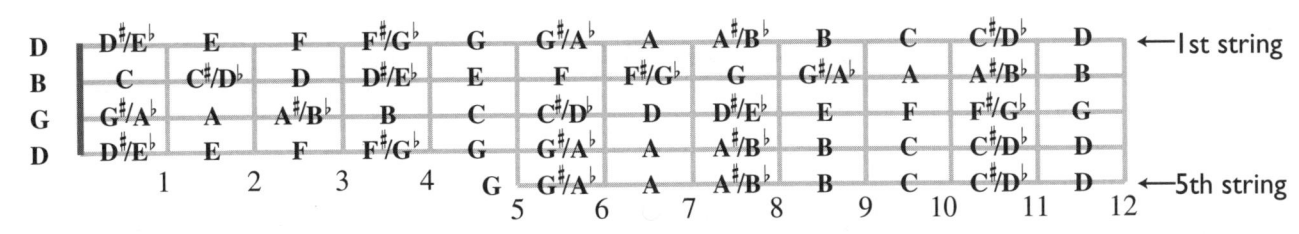

HOLDING THE BANJO

Hold the banjo much like the guitar. Due to its round shape, you will want to hold it between your legs, resting on the thighs. You can also use a strap that wraps around the *pot* or clips on to the *brackets*. It is important to hold the banjo in such a way that you are not supporting the neck with your left hand. This will allow you maximum freedom of movement.

Seated

Standing using a Strap

OPEN CHORDS IN G TUNING

Here are some chord fingerings for G tuning on the banjo.

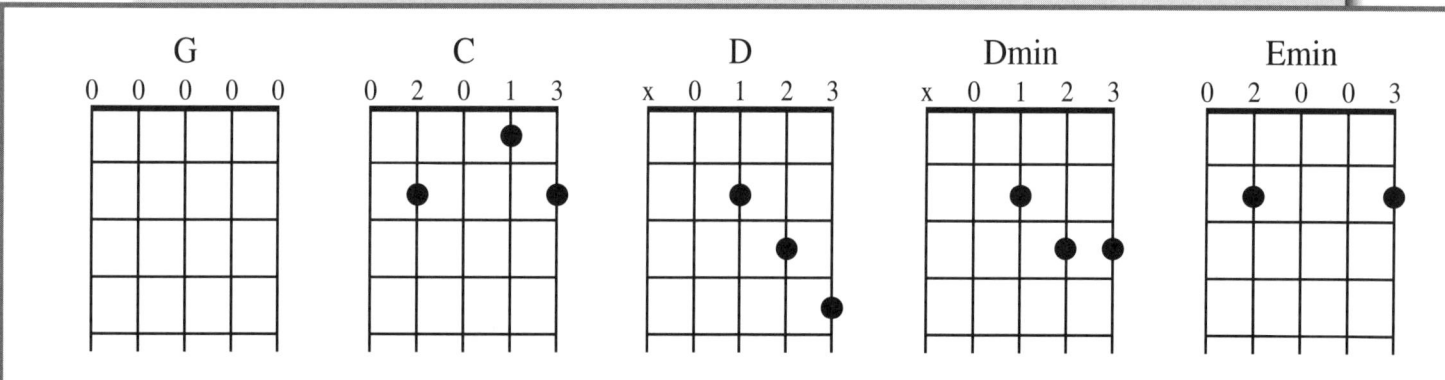

Try this chord progression using the chord fingerings you just learned. Strum in simple downstrokes with your right-hand thumb. Many banjoists use thumb picks, and you may want to try using one here (more on fingerpicks on page 52).

BOIL THEM CABBAGE DOWN (CHORDS ONLY)

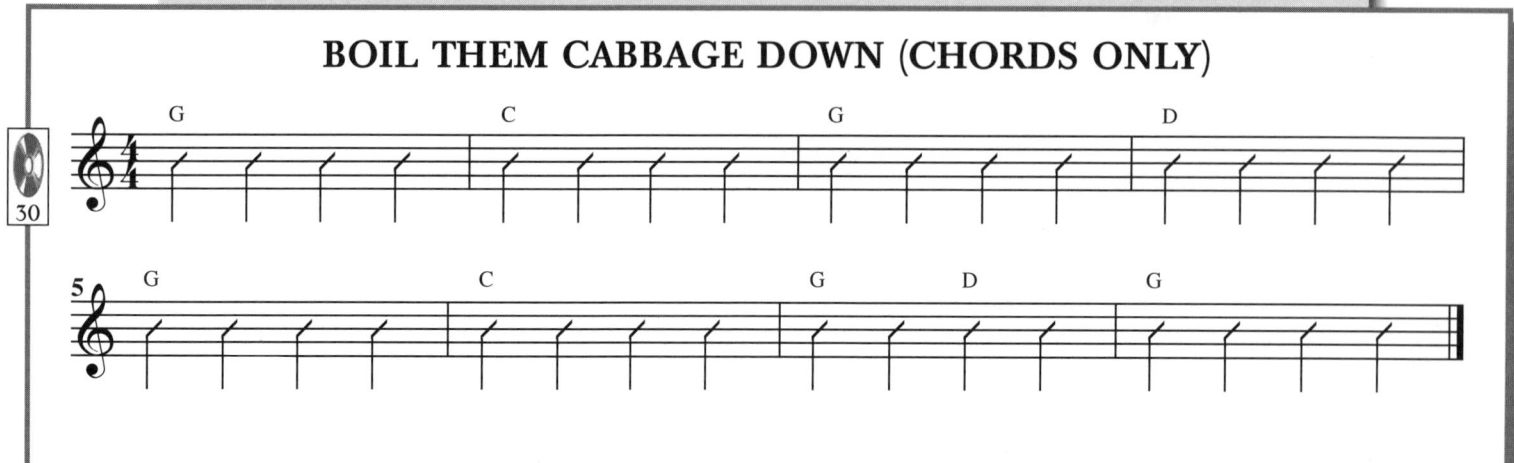

A TALE OF TWO BANJOS

There are many ways to play a banjo, but two main styles have dominated. Both styles involve a unique use of the right hand. The left-hand technique is basically identical to that used for the guitar.

CLAWHAMMER

The *clawhammer*, or old-time style most closely resembles the technique used by the African slaves who brought the banjo to America. It has a rhythmic drive and funky syncopation created by striking the strings with the back of the fingernail, and "popping" the 5th string with the thumb.

Some of the masters of the style include:
- Rich Stearns of the Horseflies
- Ralph Stanley
- Fred Cockeram
- Marcy Marxer
- David Holt

THREE-FINGER

The *three-finger*, or "bluegrass," style involves a more conventional fingerpicking technique using the thumb, index and middle fingers of the right hand. Most often played with fingerpicks, this technique creates the rolling drive in bluegrass, and also accommodates well both fluid Celtic or jazz-influenced leads.

Masters of the three-finger style include:
- Earl Scruggs, whose much-imitated style has been a key element of bluegrass since the 1940s
- Bill Keith, developer of the "melodic" style
- Béla Fleck
- John Hartford
- Tony Trishka, author of *Banjo for Beginners*, also published by the National Guitar Workshop and Alfred.

The following two chapters discuss the techniques of each style.

*The extraordinary songwriter ("Gentle on My Mind"), banjoist, fiddler, riverboat pilot and dancer **John Hartford** was a beloved and hugely influential musician. His passing in 2001 was a profound loss to the acoustic music community.*

CHAPTER 5
BANJO: CLAWHAMMER STYLE

The five-string banjo is an American instrument with West African roots. Early banjos used gourds with animal-skin heads and had a deep, plunky sound. The banjo developed into an extremely popular instrument during the nineteenth century due to its use in traveling minstrel and medicine shows. The techniques used by African slaves and by black and white minstrel performers were retained and developed by early twentieth century players in the Appalachian Mountains. These are the roots of the clawhammer style, also known as "old-time banjo," and "frailing."

DAMPENING: PUT A SOCK IN IT
Clawhammer style can be played on any five-string banjo, but many players like to use an open-back banjo, or remove the resonator of a bluegrass banjo. Old-time players also spend a lifetime trying out different tricks for muting the inside of the head. These can range from plastic bags stuffed between the dowel rod and head; to rags, baloney sandwiches and old socks. The purpose is to dampen the ringing sound of the banjo and get more "plunk."

THE CLAWHAMMER TECHNIQUE

The clawhammer technique is simple to explain: "Make a claw, then hammer with it"—in other words, curve your index finger (i) into a kind of claw, then stick your thumb out hitch-hiker style. Play melody notes by down-picking the string with the *back* of your fingernail. It is a motion much like knocking on a door. Try playing these open strings using downstrokes with the back of your index fingernail.

i = The right-hand index finger

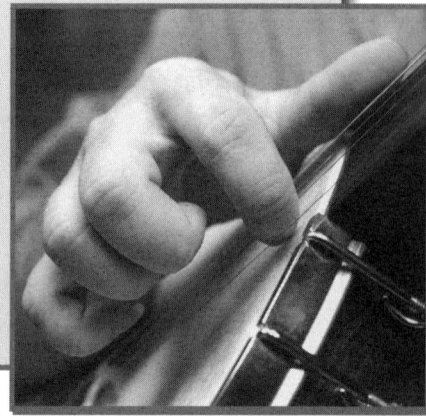

BEGINNING TIPS:
1. Keep your finger curved and try to move only from your wrist. You don't want to try to play by flexing your finger in and out, but rather by moving your hand up and down in a "knocking" motion.

2. As you play each note, allow your fingernail to rest on the next string. On the first string, don't worry if your nail comes down and hits the head.

3. Some players like to play with their right hand up over the end of the neck, where there is no banjo head. This provides a sweeter, plunkier sound and prevents you from hitting the head. Other players like the brighter and more percussive sound of hitting the head.

ADDING THE THUMB

The thumb's job in this style is to "pop" the 5th string between the downstrokes of the claw finger. Here's how to do it:

1. Play a melody note on the open 1st string with a downstroke of your index finger, then *stop–do not move*! Your thumb ("*T*") should be resting on the 5th string and your index finger should be close to, or touching, the head.
2. Without flexing your finger or moving your thumb, raise your hand back up from your wrist. This will cause the thumb to "pop" off the 5th string, setting it ringing.
3. Try this as a two-step motion: claw–pop, claw–pop. Make the move from your arm and wrist with minimal movement of the finger and thumb. Here are some exercises using open strings. Also try mixing these up and adding fretted notes.

T = Thumb

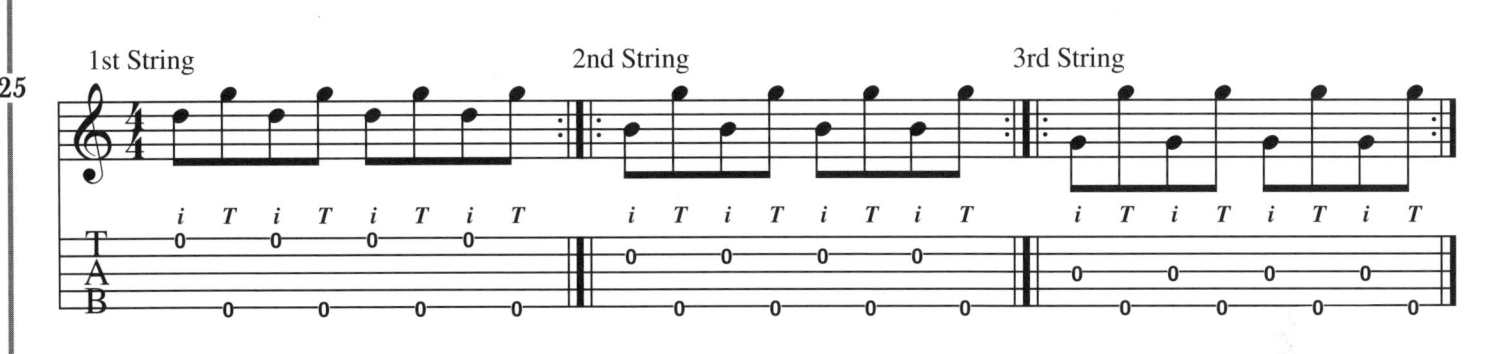

FRAILING, THE BRUSHSTROKE, OR "BUMP-DITTY-BOOM-CHICKA"

You will find that much of the time, we simply use the claw-and-pop move you just learned. Sometimes, you can add a *brush stroke*. This is done by using the remaining fingers (the middle and ring fingers) to brush lightly across the first two or three strings of the banjo. The brush is often incorporated between a melody note ("claw") and a thumb note ("pop"). When done properly, you will create a steady, galloping rhythm that sounds like "bump-ditty, bump-ditty," or "boom-chicka, boom-chicka." This rhythm mimics the bluegrass "shuffle" rhythm (an eighth and two sixteenths) used by fiddlers. Commonly, and for the purposes of this book, this move is called *frailing*. The brush is indicated by a downward arrow ↓. Try the move with the following examples.

↓ = Brush

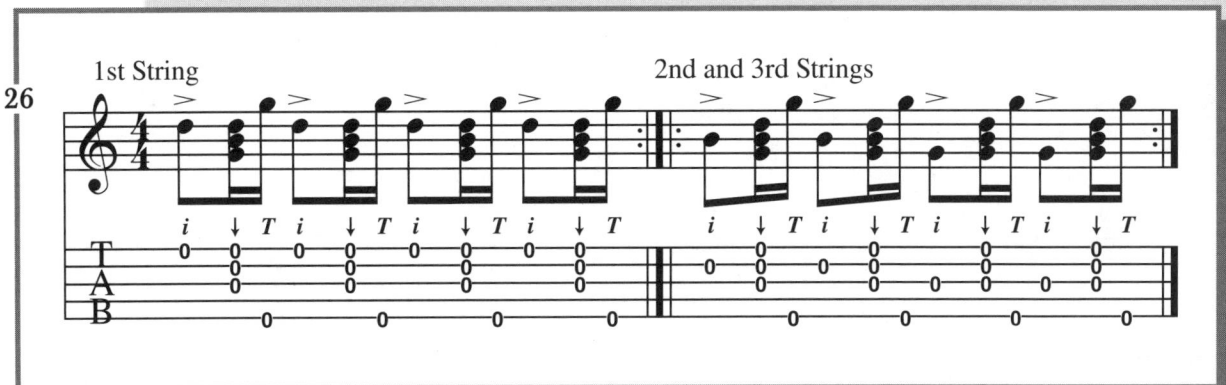

Now, let's incorporate the frailing rhythm pattern with a few basic chords to play that old chestnut folk song, "Boil Them Cabbage Down." Play slowly and try to hit the melody notes (the notes played with *i*) as accurately and solidly as possible. As you improve at this, try to bring out the melody notes and play the brushes and thumb notes a bit softer.

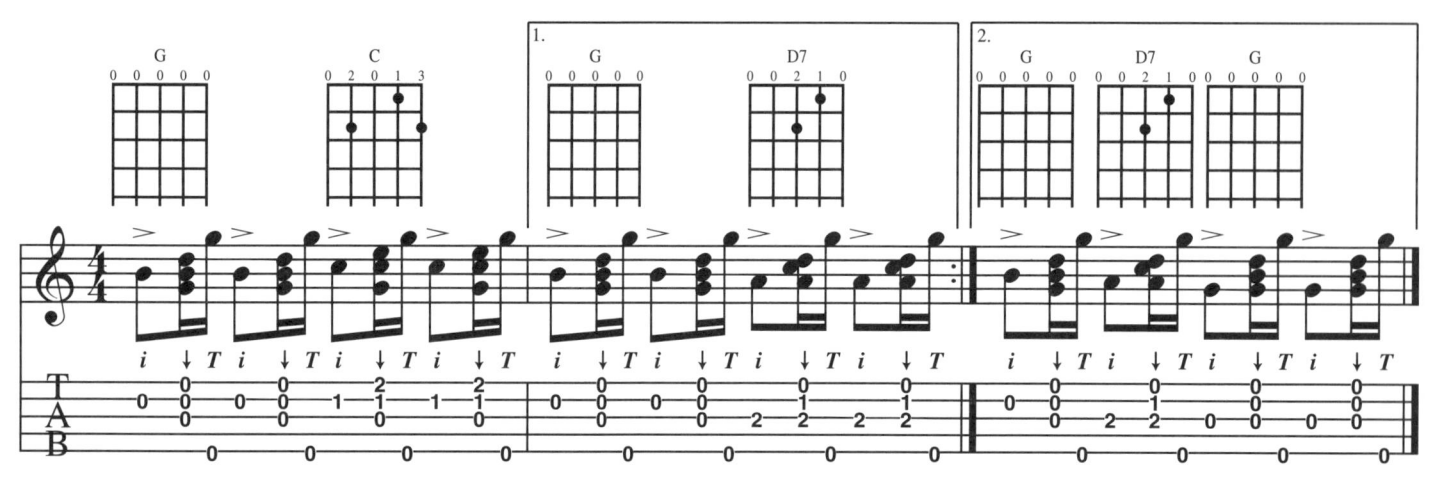

HAMMER-ONS AND PULL-OFFS

As you may have noticed, the frailing and clawhammer rhythm can be a little restrictive and repetitive. Part of the fun of the style is figuring out ways to get around the insistent shuffle rhythm of frailing. The first step is to incorporate hammer-ons and pull-offs with your left hand. These are done the same way as on the guitar. When you perform a hammer-on, remember to bring the left-hand finger down with enough speed and accuracy to sound the note as if it had been plucked. Pull-offs should be done with a small snap of the finger in order to sound the note clearly.

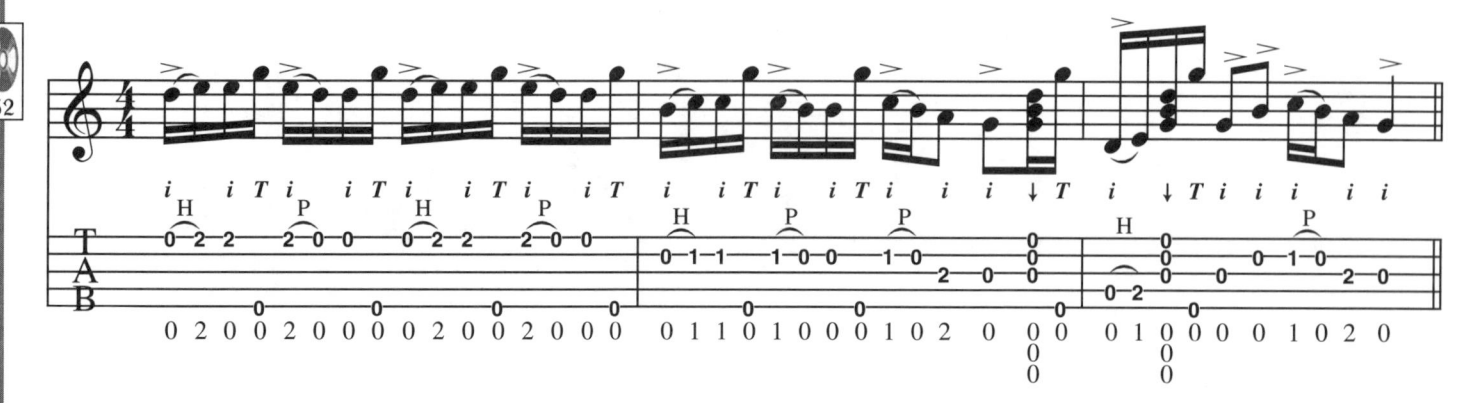

Here is a simple version of "Old Joe Clark" using all the techniques you have learned so far. Work slowly and patiently!

Special Jamming Note: This tune is most commonly played in the key of A (see the mandolin version on page 21). The traditional banjo approach is to play "A" tunes in the G tuning. You must then tune your banjo up a whole step, or use a capo at the 2nd fret along with a spike or 5th string capo at the 7th fret. You may also tune the 5th string up one whole step to A to match the tuning created by the capo. This version is notated in open position in the key of G.

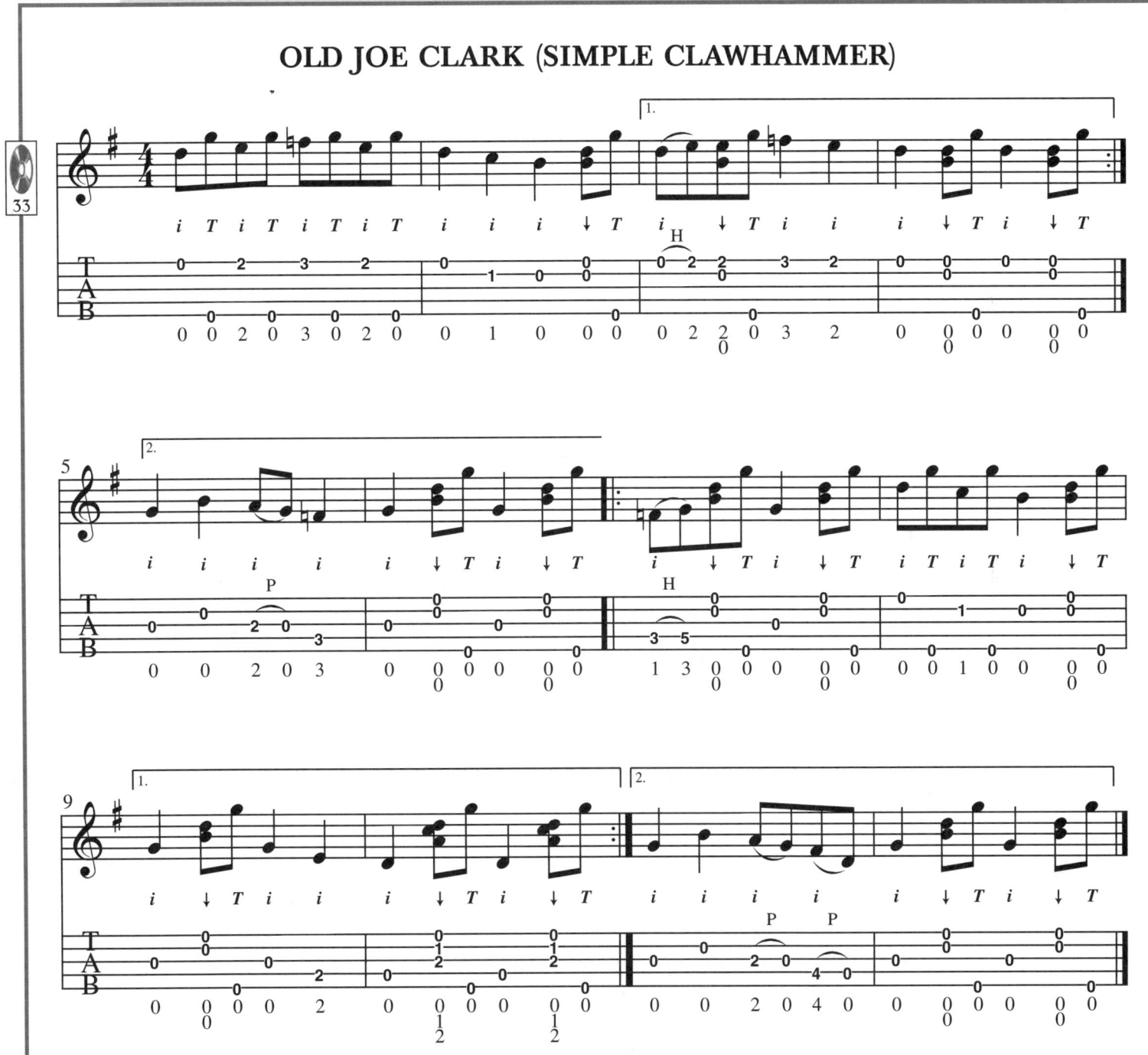

The Multi-Instrumental Guitarist • 45

DROP THUMB, OR "MELODIC" CLAWHAMMER

Another technique for expanding your rhythmic and melodic possibilities is the *drop thumb*. With this technique, you will move the thumb down to the other strings and use the "popping" motion to play melodic notes as well as the rhythmic drone on the 5th string. This technique is more advanced and requires that you be very comfortable with the standard moves. Try the following exercises.

PRACTICE NOTE:
Try doing these examples one measure at a time, repeating each measure over and over. When you are comfortable with each new move, start stringing them together.

Simple Drop Thumb Exercise

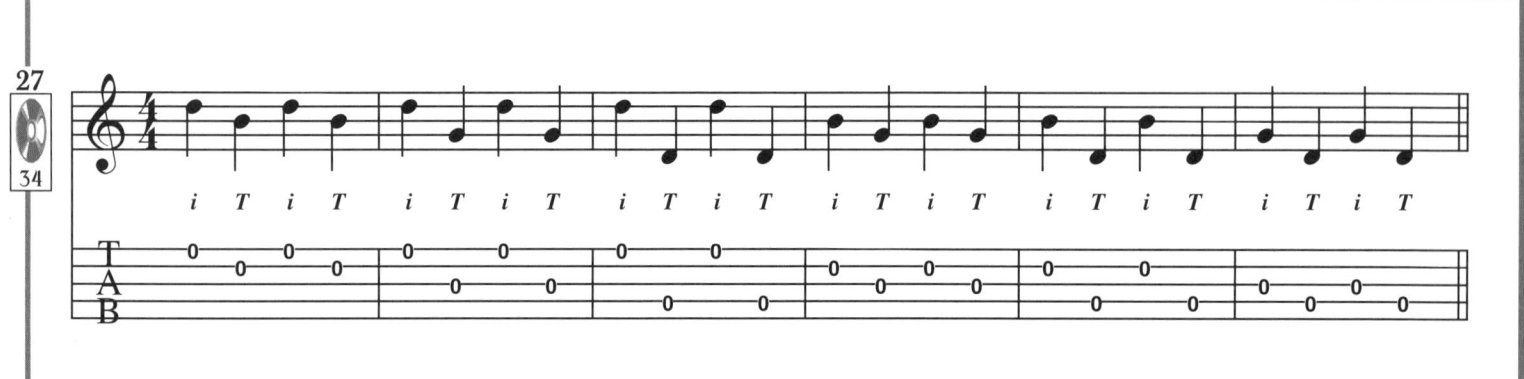

Advanced Drop Thumb Exercise

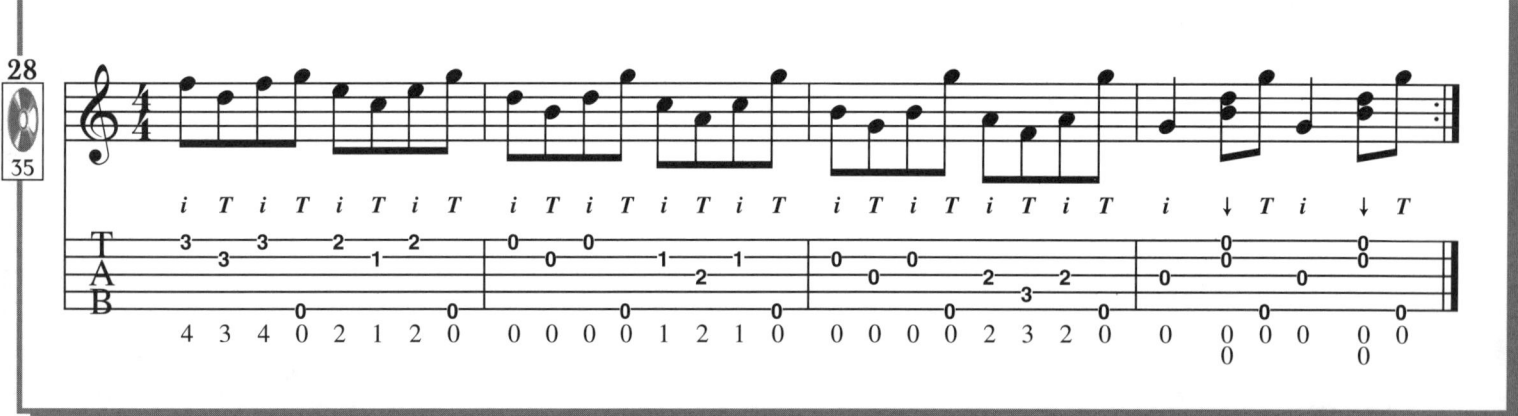

46 • The Multi-Instrumental Guitarist

Now try this more advanced version of "Old Joe Clark." It incorporates drop thumb technique along with hammer-ons, pull-offs and slides. This style attempts to capture more of the same notes that a fiddler might play, and therefore is called the *melodic clawhammer style*. Keep in mind that this tune is traditionally set in the key of A, so you will need to capo or tune up to jam with other players.

OLD JOE CLARK (MELODIC CLAWHAMMER)

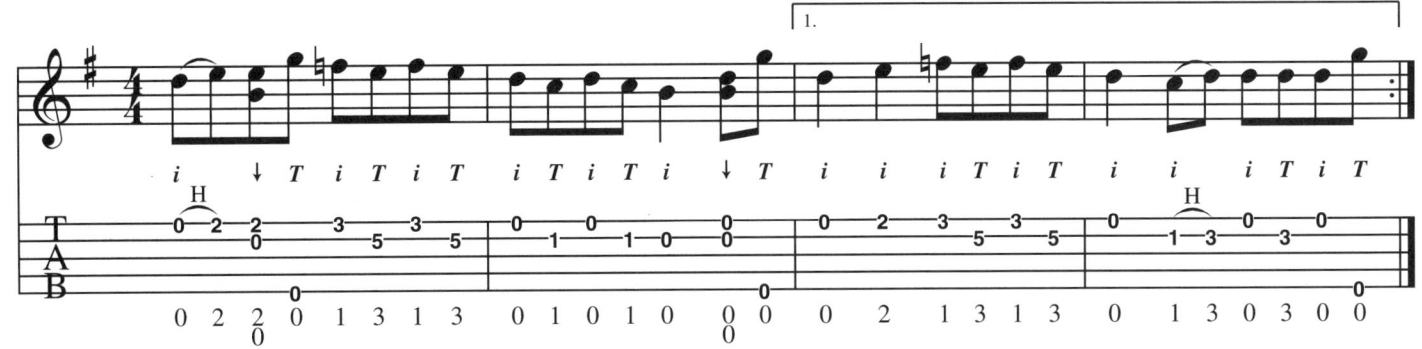

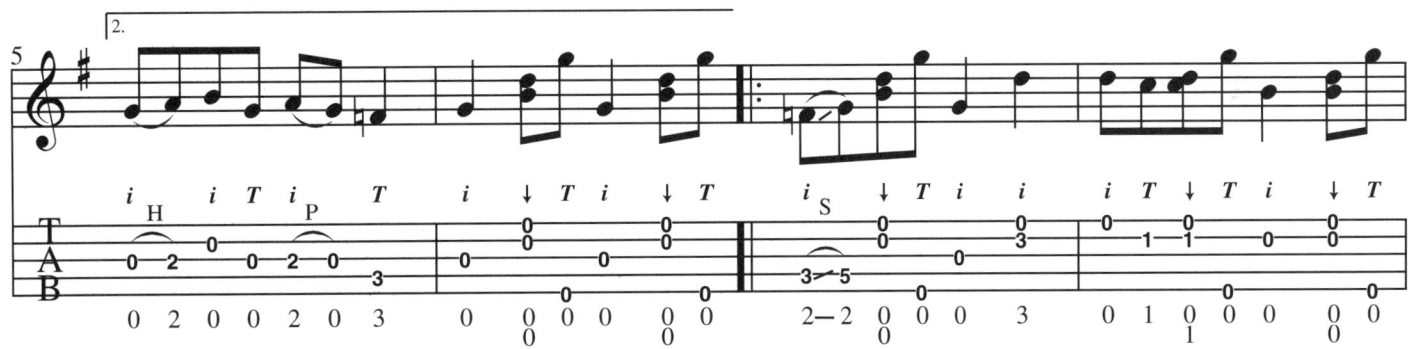

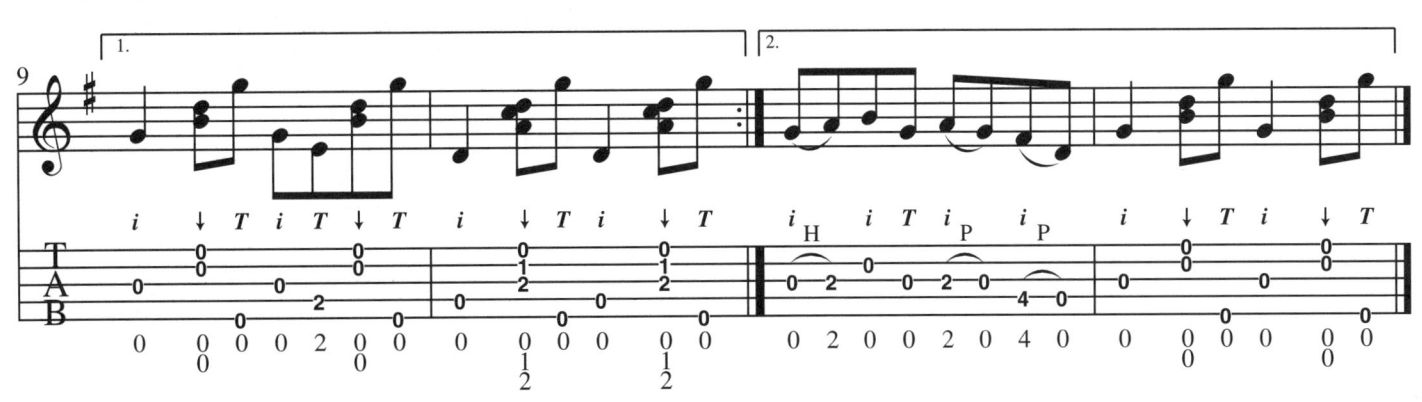

The Multi-Instrumental Guitarist • 47

MODAL TUNING

In the old-time tradition, a *modal* tune is any tune using a minor, Dorian, Mixolydian or blues scale. These scales have in common the lowered seventh scale degree (♭7), as well as various other alterations of the major scale. Clawhammer banjo has a special tuning used just for this sound. This tuning is based on G tuning, with the 2nd string raised one half step to C. This tuning is called *modal tuning*, *sawmill tuning* or *mountain minor* tuning. Here are the notes and matching frets.

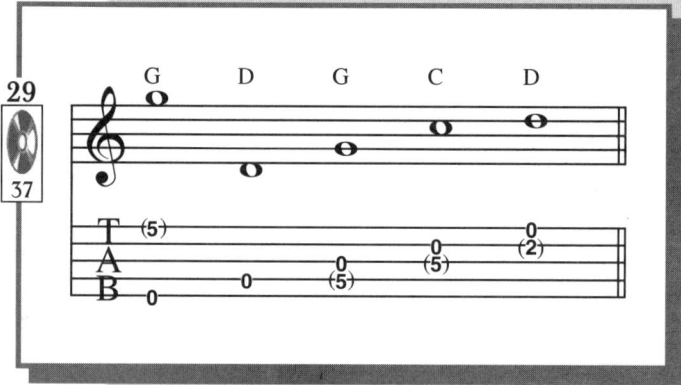

THE MINOR PENTATONIC SCALE IN MODAL TUNING

Below is a G Minor pentatonic scale that is often used in modal tuning. It also makes a great scale for playing blues.

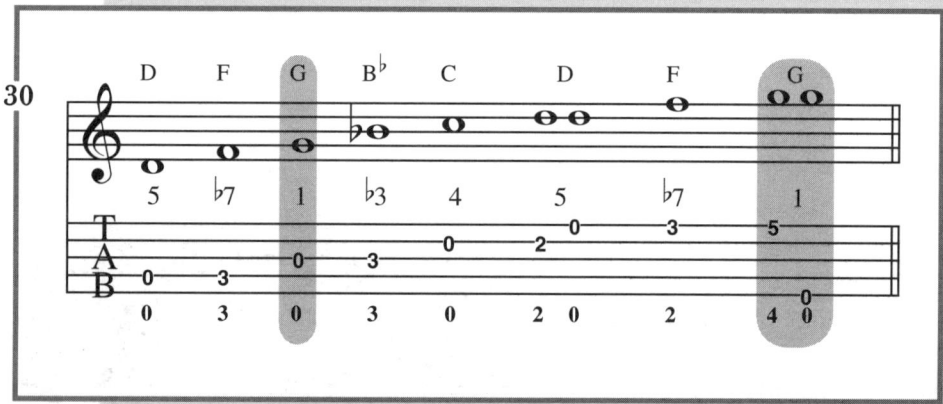

48 • The Multi-Instrumental Guitarist

Try this version of "Shady Grove." It is especially fun to play in the clawhammer style. Like "Old Joe Clark," this tune is traditionally played in the key of A. Most of the "modal" fiddle tunes are in the key of A, requiring banjo players to use a capo or a higher tuning. See the Special Jamming Note for "Old Joe Clark" page 45. This version is shown in modal tuning without a capo.

SHADY GROVE

Musician, singer, songwriter, folklorist, labor activist, environmentalist and peace advocate **Pete Seeger** *was born in Patterson, New York in 1919. He is a highly visible and much beloved figure in American life. He has made some one hundred recordings, written and collaborated on numerous songbooks and technical manuals on playing the banjo.*

PHOTO • BILL KROPF

The Multi-Instrumental Guitarist • 49

C TUNING

For many clawhammer players, this tuning is more standard than G tuning. It is used to play tunes in the key of C, and even more often used with a capo to play tunes in the key of D. Here are the notes and matching frets for C tuning.

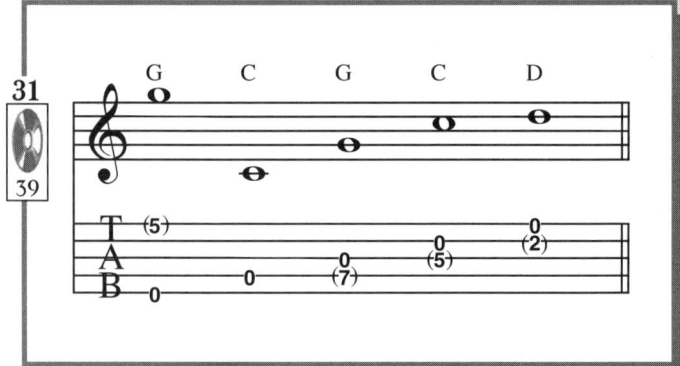

Special Jamming Note on Playing in D:

A huge number of old-time fiddle and banjo tunes are in the key of D. Use either of these methods to play these tunes in their proper key.

1. Tune the banjo to C tuning, then capo the 2nd fret. Also raise the 5th string by using a spike or capo at the 7th fret, or by tuning the string up one whole step.

2. Tune the whole banjo up to D tuning, which is one whole step higher than C tuning. The notes from the 5th string to the first are (using lowercase letters for high notes): a–D–A–d–e.

BASIC CHORDS IN C TUNING

Below are the basic chords for C tuning. They are also labeled I, IV, V and vi to show their relationships with the basic key of C. This will help you when you use this tuning with a capo to play in D.

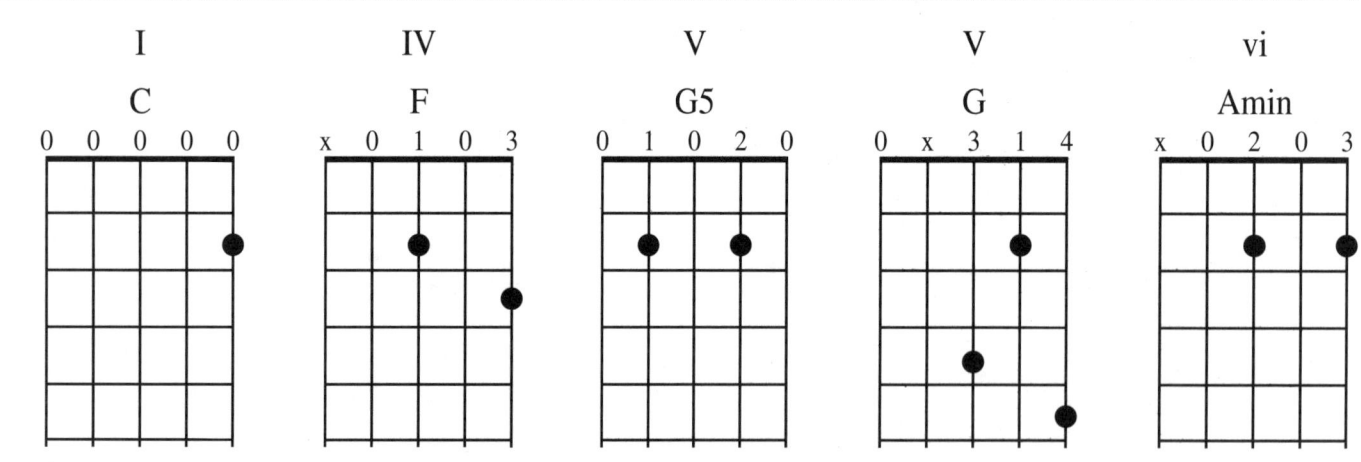

Roman Numeral Review
Uppercase = Major chords
Lowercase = Minor Chords

I or i........1	V or v......5
II or ii.....2	VI or vi...6
III or iii...3	VI or vi...7
IV or iv...4	

50 • The Multi-Instrumental Guitarist

This is a version of the popular jamming tune "Soldier's Joy." It is shown in open position, C tuning. To jam with others in the traditional key of D, capo at the 2nd fret and raise the 5th string to A (using spikes, a 5th string capo, or just tune it up).

CHAPTER 6
BANJO: THREE-FINGER STYLE

The three-finger, or bluegrass, style developed in the early twentieth century as an extension of two-finger picking. The two-finger style, which can be heard in the playing of modern master Will Keyes, is similar to clawhammer in feel, but uses a more traditional upstroke with the fingers. In the 1940s, players such as Earl Scruggs and Snuffy Jenkins emerged incorporating a third right-hand finger to create *rolls* (broken chords). This is by far the most commonly heard five-string banjo style; it is heard in bluegrass, country and even rock music.

Unless otherwise noted, the examples in this chapter will be in G tuning (page 39), which is the most common tuning for three-finger style banjo.

FINGERPICKS

Three-finger style is traditionally played with fingerpicks. While not an absolute requirement, they do provide the consistent, even tone, and the powerful "bang" that bluegrass banjo is known for. The standard setup is a plastic thumbpick and two metal fingerpicks. There are many styles available. Experiment until you find the kinds and sizes that work for you.

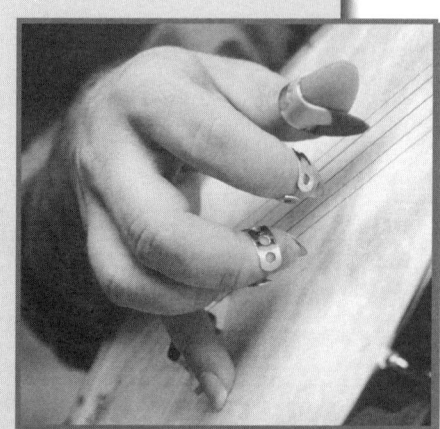

Most players rotate the wrist slightly to position the fingerpicks perpendicular to the strings. It is also common to anchor the pinky finger to the head of the banjo, providing a stable position and allowing you to "dig in" for more volume and speed. Guitarists coming from a fingerstyle or classical background may find that a floating hand position is stable enough. That is just fine! Don't let the banjo pros scare you into cramping up a well-honed position. Either way will work, as long as the tone is there.

THREE BASIC BANJO ROLLS

Three-finger-style banjo uses endless combinations and variations of three basic picking patterns, or rolls. These same patterns are also heard in lap slide and steel playing.

FORWARD ROLLS
The *forward roll* is a three-note pattern that goes "thumb–index–middle" or *T–i–m*. It can be launched with (led by) any of the three fingers, but usually kicks off with the index or thumb. Try these examples. Repeat each one many times to practice steady rhythm and keeping a full tone.

52 • The Multi-Instrumental Guitarist

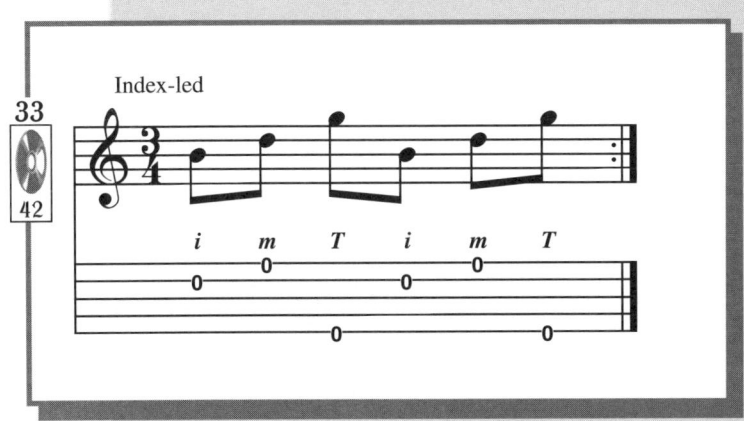

You can use the forward roll and some basic chords to play the classic "Boil Them Cabbage Down." Note that the roll starts over again (the pattern begins again) on each new chord. Also watch out for the chord switch halfway through measure 7.

BOIL THEM CABBAGE DOWN INTO CABBAGE ROLLS

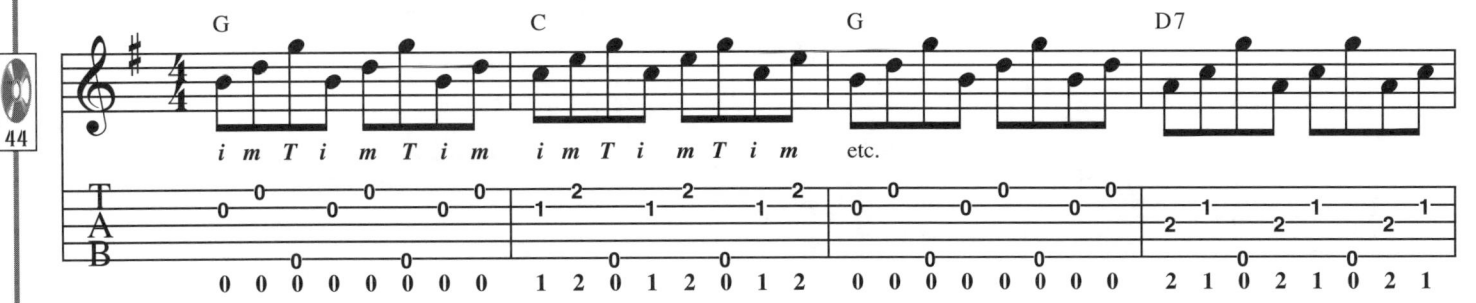

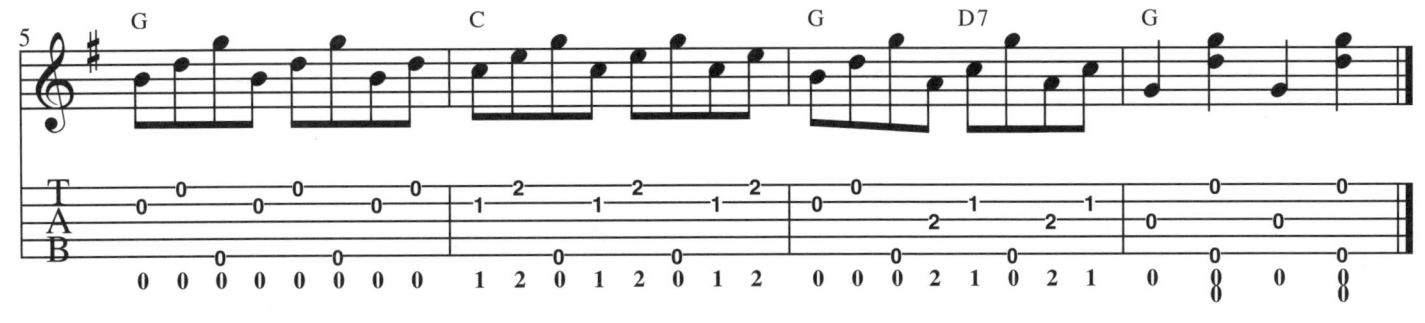

The Multi-Instrumental Guitarist • 53

BACKWARD ROLL

The *backward roll* is just like the forward roll, only the order of the index and middle fingers is reversed: *T–m–i*. The *T* or *i* are still most likely to kick it off. Try the following examples. Work slowly and steadily. Try to play all the notes at the same volume.

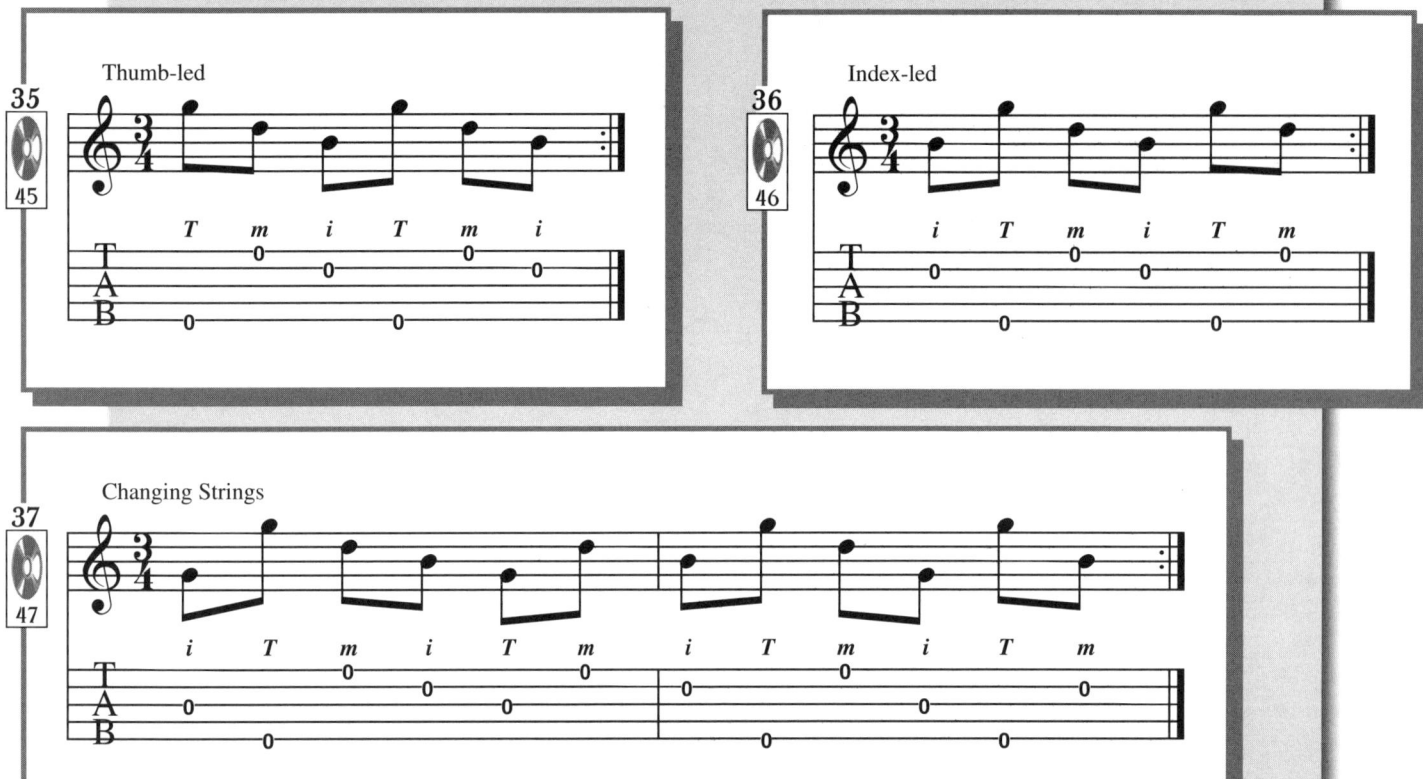

SQUARE ROLL

In a *square roll*, the main feature is the thumb alternating with the fingers. This can happen in numerous combinations. Here are a few examples.

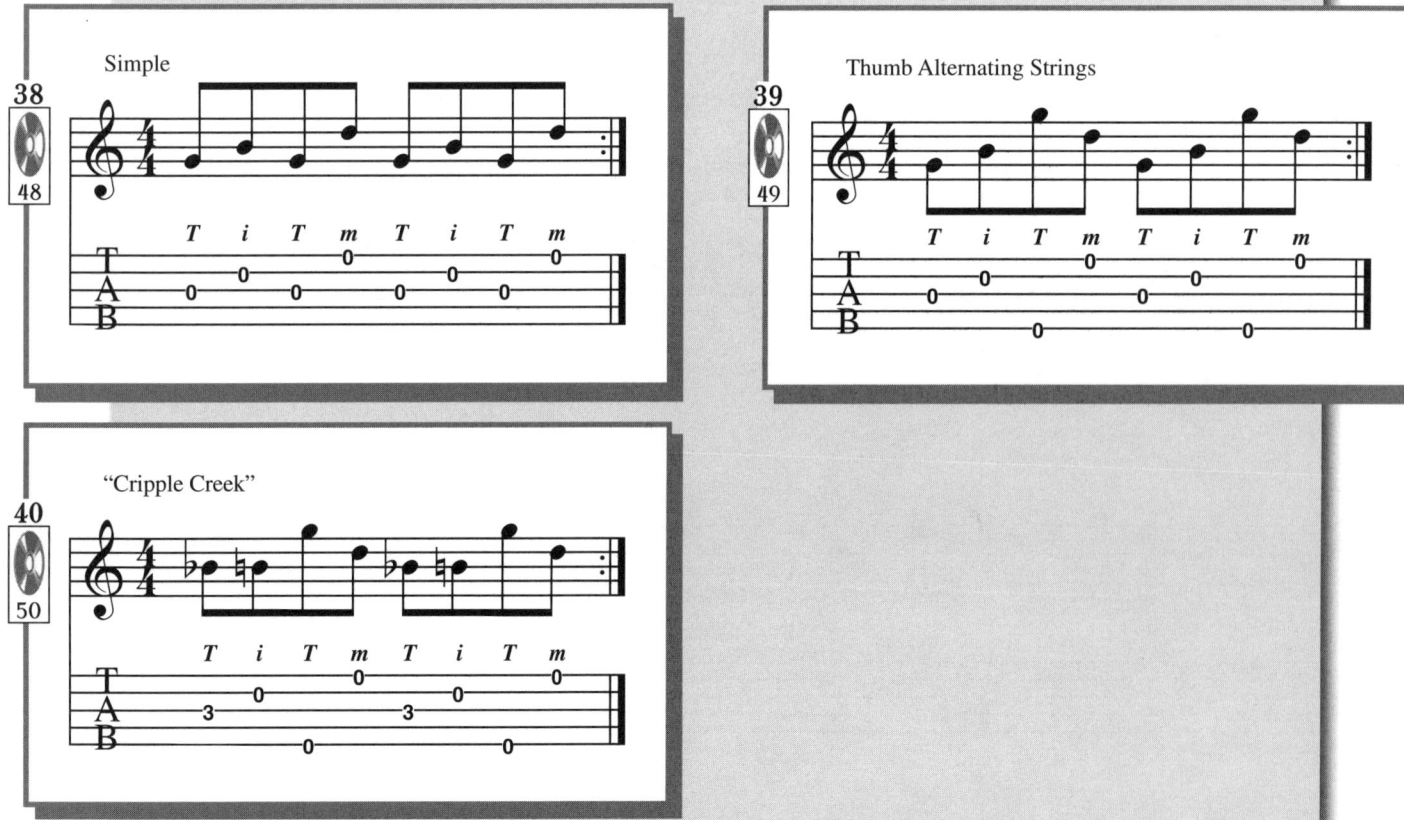

54 • The Multi-Instrumental Guitarist

No introduction to the three-finger style banjo is complete without the song "Cripple Creek." This tune incorporates slides, hammer-ons, pull-offs and rolls. Play slowly and work on each measure separately, adding another measure as each one is mastered. Chords have been included.

Notice that this tune is cut time ¢, which is felt in two. In cut time, or $\frac{2}{2}$; a half note equals one beat, a quarter note equals half of a beat, and there are two beats to the measure. This is essentially a way of saying that the tempo is quite fast and it should feel like it has two "big" beats per measure rather than four.

♪ = *Grace note.* These small, ornamental notes are played quickly, just before the main note, in this case, on the beat.

BACKUP BANJO

The rolling, banging banjo provides much of the drive in bluegrass music. However, you can increase the thrill factor of your banjo brilliance in a band by incorporating other textures and allowing other instruments to get a word in edgewise. Think of it as a form of musical generosity. This is known as playing *backup*.

One technique that will help you is the use of movable chord forms. Like barre chords on the guitar, these allow you to play chords in a variety of places on the neck and work the range of the instrument to your advantage. In the following chord forms, the root has been identified with an "R" so that you can easily locate on the fingerboard the specific chord you need. Note that these forms do not use open strings, and the 5th string should be avoided.

MOVABLE CHORD FORMS

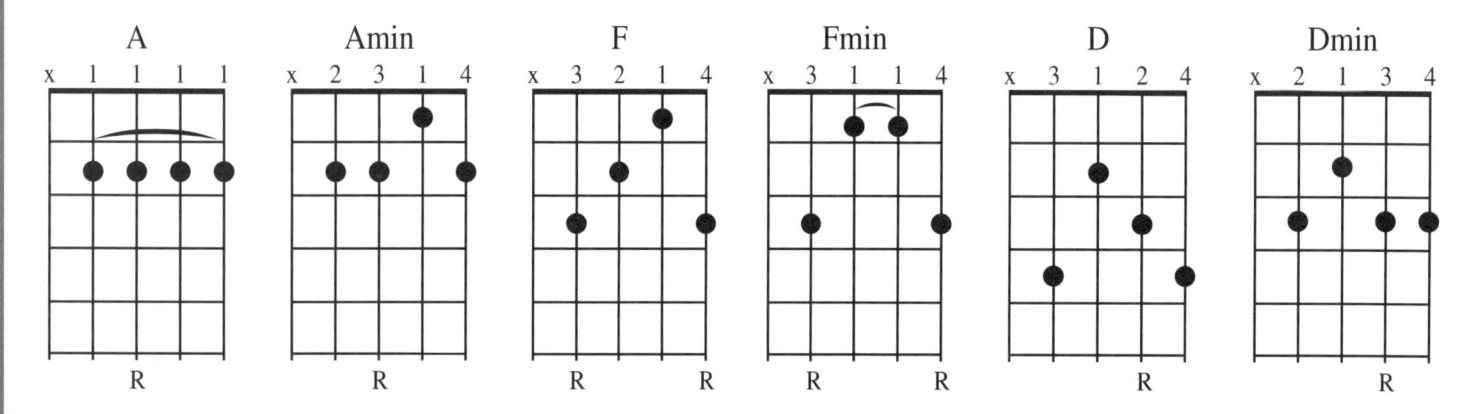

BACKUP PATTERNS

Below are two backup rhythm patterns you can use. The first mimics the "boom-chick" rhythm often used by the mandolin. The second is a variation that sounds like "boom-a-chick." On the "chick" parts of these patterns (beats 2 and 4), make the notes short by relaxing the pressure in your left-hand fingers but keeping them on the strings. This is called playing *staccato*, and is indicated with a dot over the note or notes.

Backup Pattern No. 1

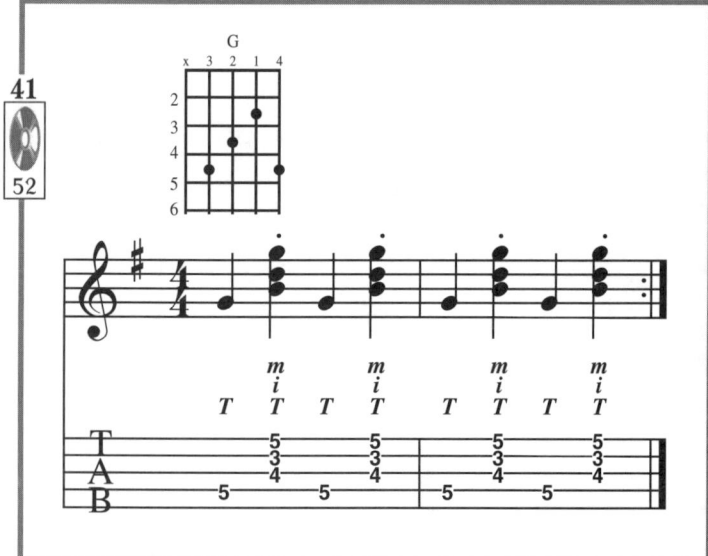

Backup Pattern No. 2

Now try the backup chords to the blues and bluegrass traditional classic "Sittin' on Top of the World." Note that the backup pattern used here combines the two you have just learned.

SITTIN' ON TOP OF THE WORLD (BACKUP BANJO)

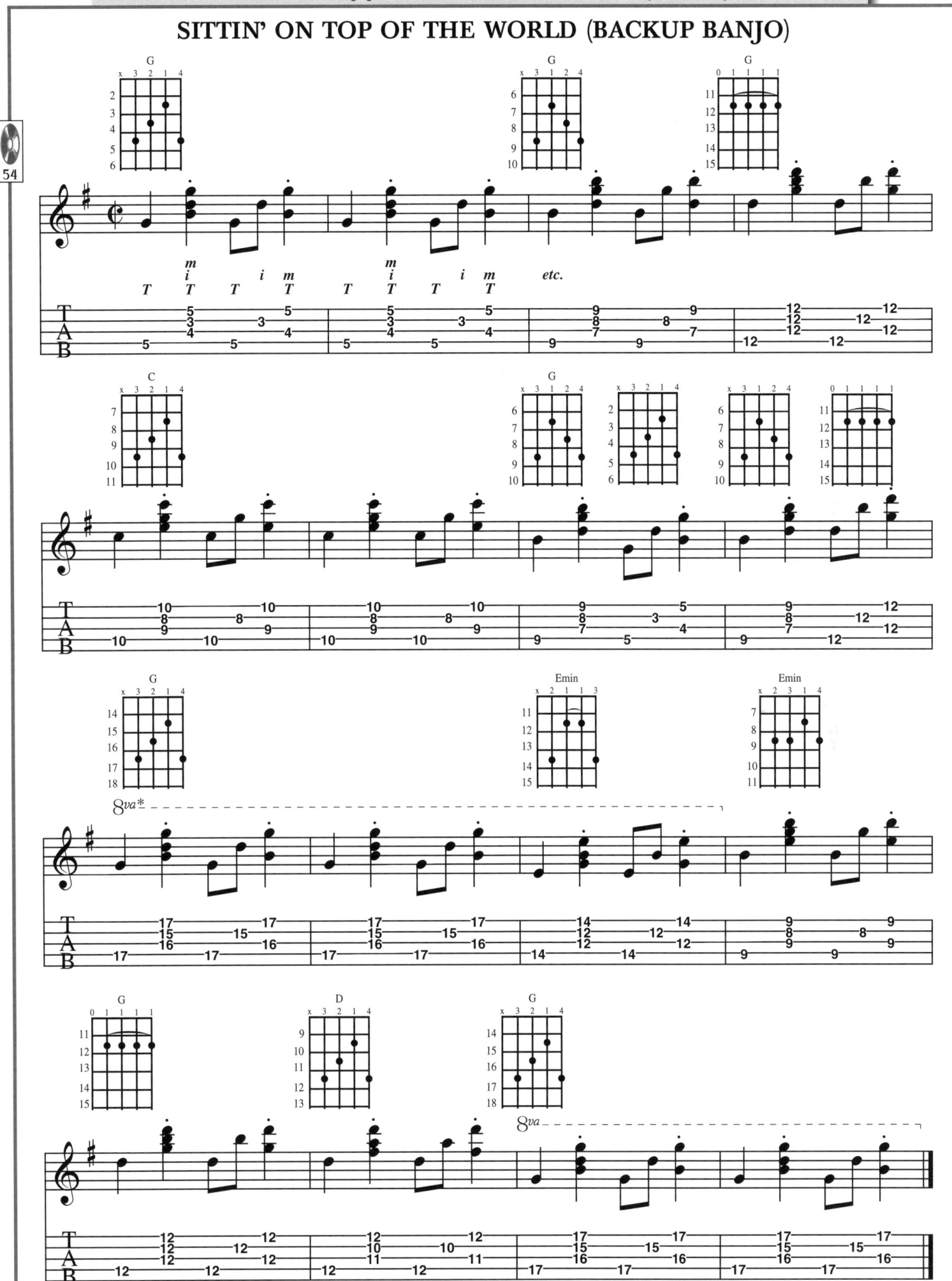

*8va means to play one octave higher than written.

PUTTING THE BLUES IN YOUR BLUEGRASS

One of the most influential banjo pickers of all time is Earl Scruggs. Scruggs combines a rolling banjo style with guitar-like blues licks and funky syncopation to create the definitive sound of three-finger style banjo. His open, humorous good nature shone through in his years of partnership with guitarist Lester Flatt as "Flatt and Scruggs," and continues to entertain in his more recent collaborations with artists such as Marty Stuart, Steve Martin and Billy Bob Thornton.

THE UNISON "D" ROLL

This is a signature sound of three-finger style banjo, and can be used for D or G chords. The roll involves the use of a hammer-on to the D note on the 2nd string, as well as the D on the open 1st string. Here are two common versions.

BLUES LICKS

Each of these bluesy riffs is often used as a sort of punctuation mark to end a phrase.

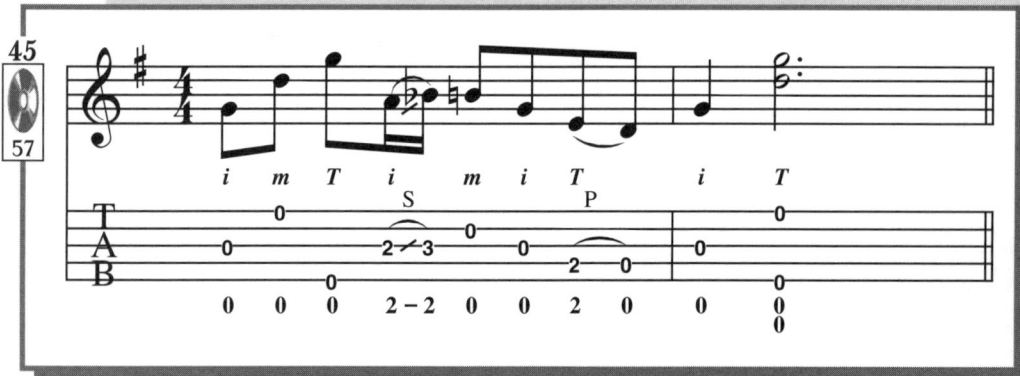

58 • The Multi-Instrumental Guitarist

Here is a full three-finger style lead banjo treatment of "Sittin' on Top of the World." As with all tunes, this one should be taken one small step at a time. Each measure of this tune provides a new move that will be useful in dozens of other tunes. Note the incorporation of bends, slides, hammer-ons, pull-offs and rolls.

SITTIN' ON TOP OF THE WORLD (LEAD BANJO)

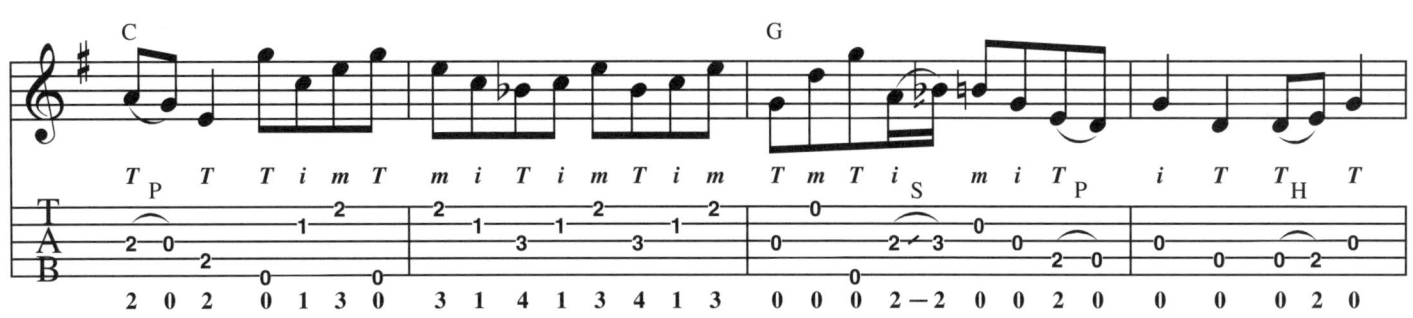

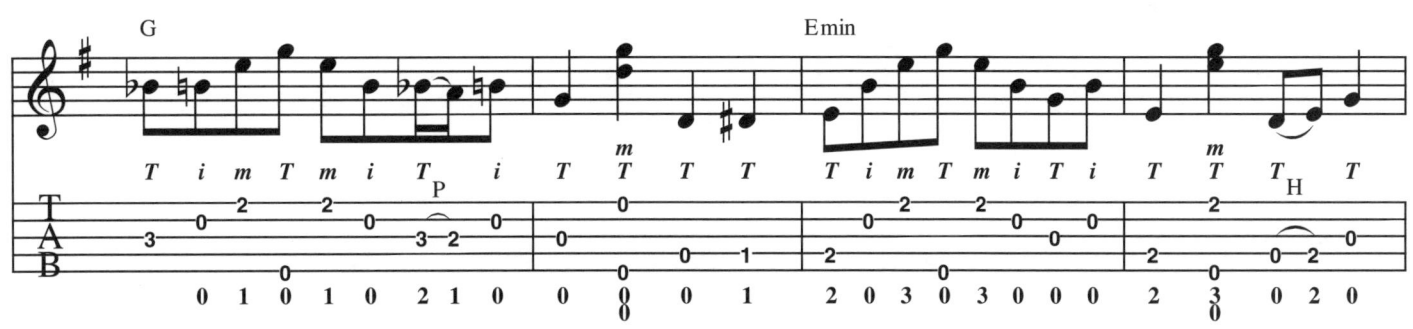

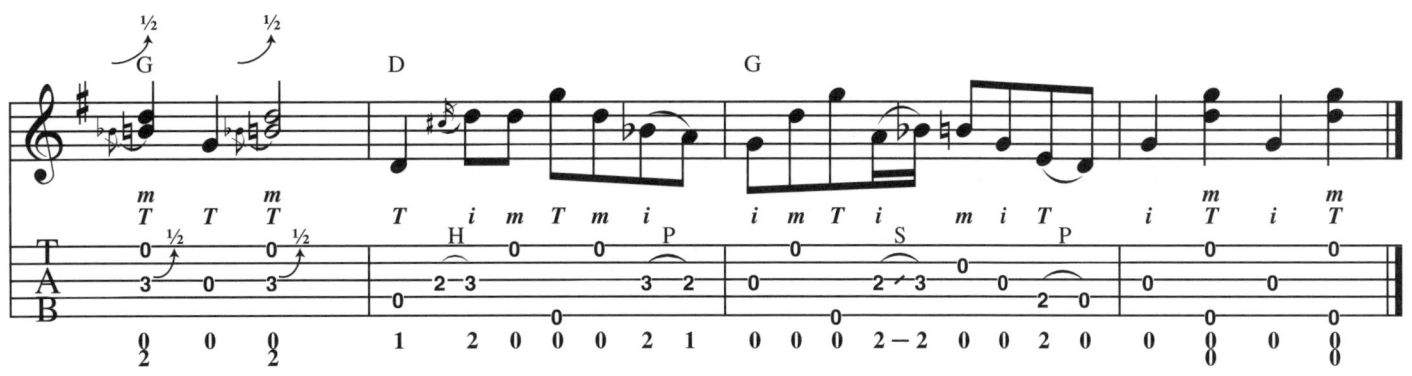

KICKOFFS AND TAGS

Every bluegrass instrument has its own vocabulary of *kickoffs* (introductions) and *tags* (endings). These can be grafted on to some of the tunes you have been working on. As you get more experienced, you will develop your own variations.

Kickoffs are used to introduce a tune and to set the pace. They take the place of "counting off" a tune verbally ("ah 1 and ah 2..."). A good kickoff should have a strong, recognizable beat. It will usually be four or eight-beats long. One of the most common forms of kickoff is often called "potatoes," because it sort of sounds like "1 potato, 2 potato, 3 potato, 4 potato." Here are a couple of "potato" patterns.

POTATOES

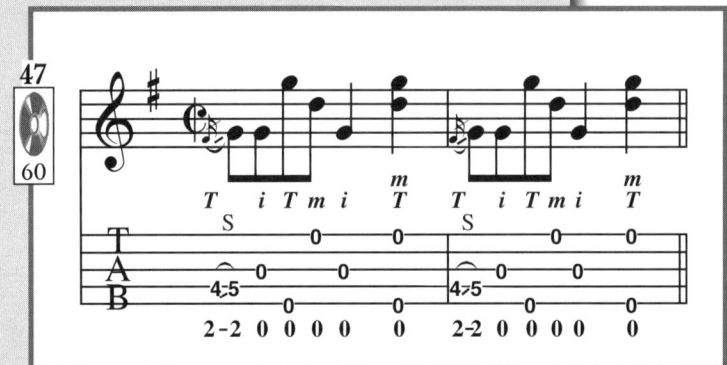

WALK-UPS

Other kickoffs give the listener some idea of where the song is going. The *walk-up*, which involves mostly stepwise movement up to the keynote of a tune, is a good example of this. For example, a song that starts of on a D note might use the walk-up to D shown in example 48. Also shown are walk-ups to low G and high G.

Walk-up to D

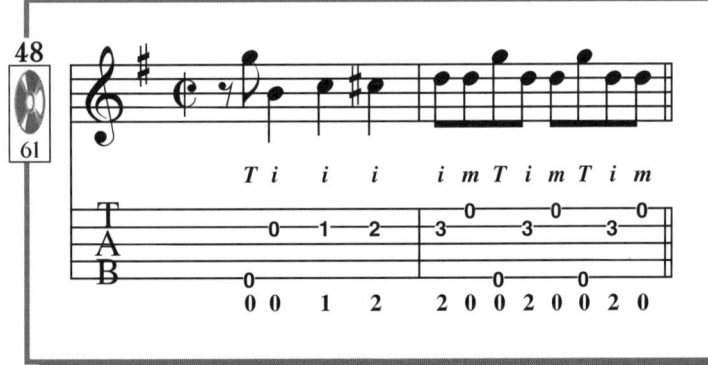

Walk-up to Low G

Walk-up to High G

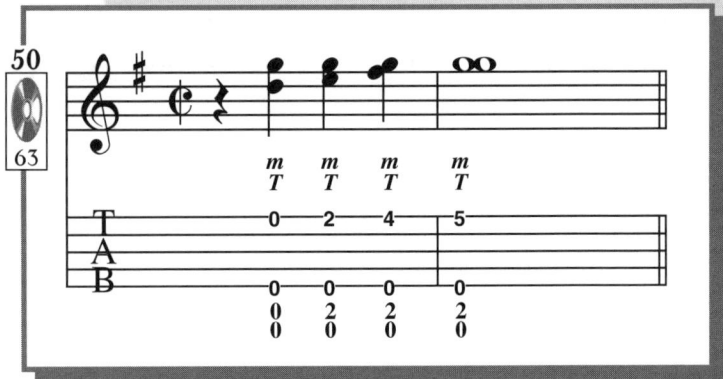

TAG: SHAVE AND A HAIRCUT

Think of the old standby "Shave and a haircut, two bits." This familiar rhythm is often attached to the end of a song as a kind of exclamation point. Tags like this give your band one last chance to end all together, and therefore create the impression that you all know what you are doing (grin).

Here are two banjo versions of "Shave and a haircut." Try adding them to your renditions of "Cripple Creek" and "Sittin' on Top of the World."

Shave and a Haircut

High Version

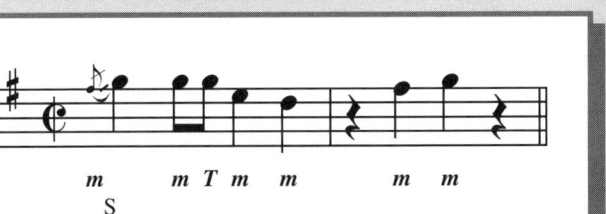
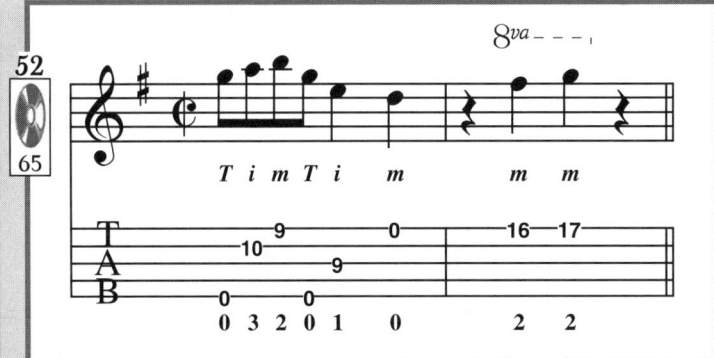

Here are two more tags that sound great on the banjo. The first is in the rolling style, and the second is in the *melodic style*, in which the notes in a stepwise passage appear on different strings and ring through one another. For more on the melodic style see, page 64.

Rolling Tag

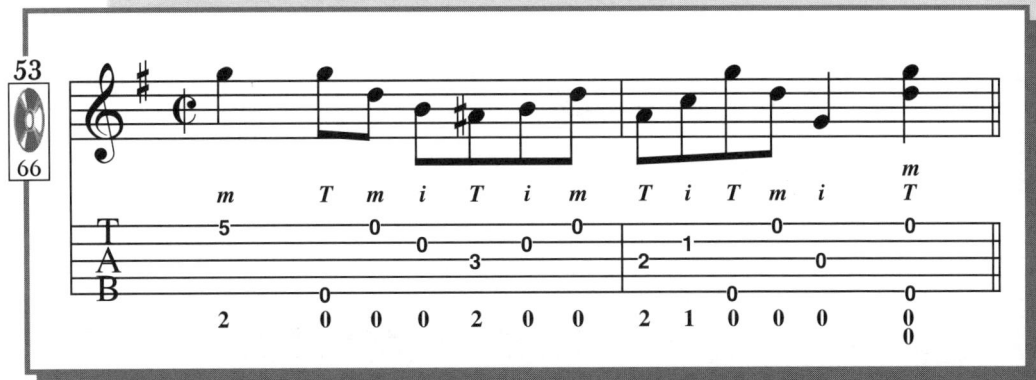

Melodic Tag

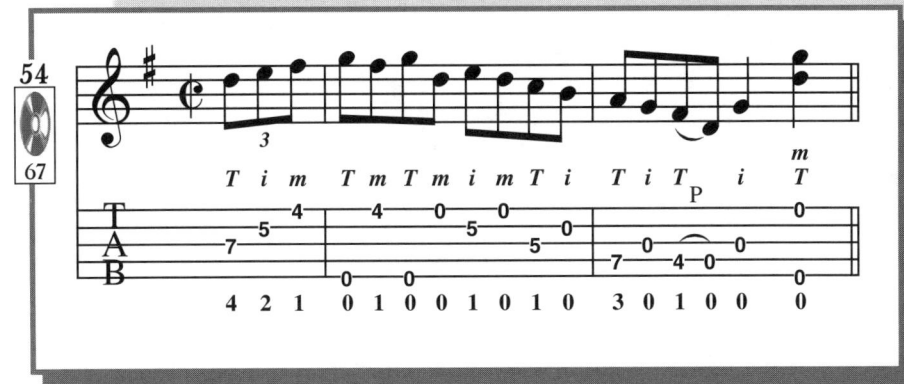

SINGLE-STRING STYLE BANJO

This style developed among players who wanted to expand the range of textures used in bluegrass banjo. Single-string style involves playing lead passages using scales and alternate picking, much like a guitar or mandolin. The acknowledged pioneer of this technique is Don Reno.

To play in the single-string style, you must learn to use your fingerpicks the way a flatpick is used on the guitar or mandolin. Downstrokes are made with the thumb and upstrokes are made with the index or middle finger. Downstrokes are played on the *onbeats* (the numbered parts of beats—1, 2, 3, 4) and upstrokes are used on the *offbeats* (the "ands" between the onbeats). Sticking rigidly to this formula will help you develop a steady rhythm and free you to focus on your left hand and improvisation, rather than on how to pick the notes.

Try these exercises to get you started; then, make up more in this style.

Single-String Exercises

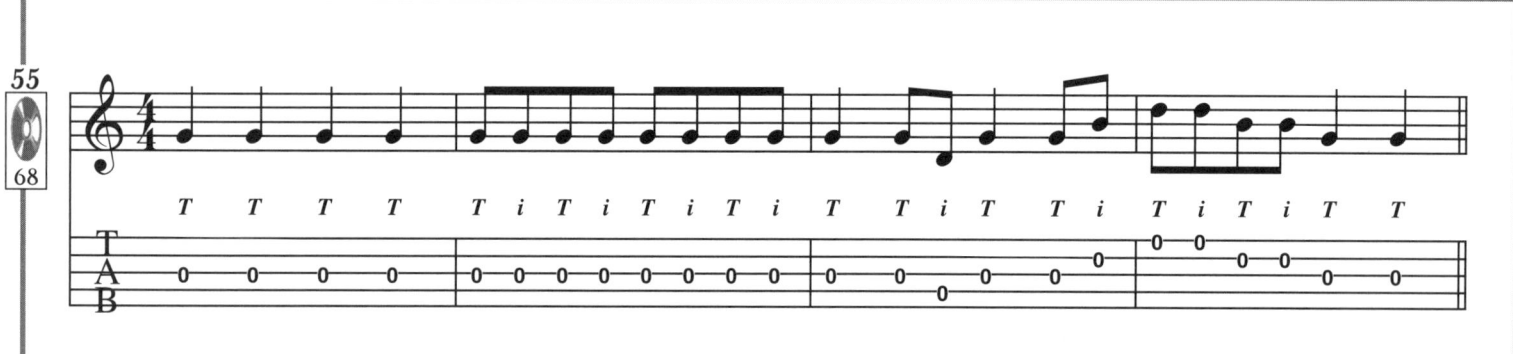

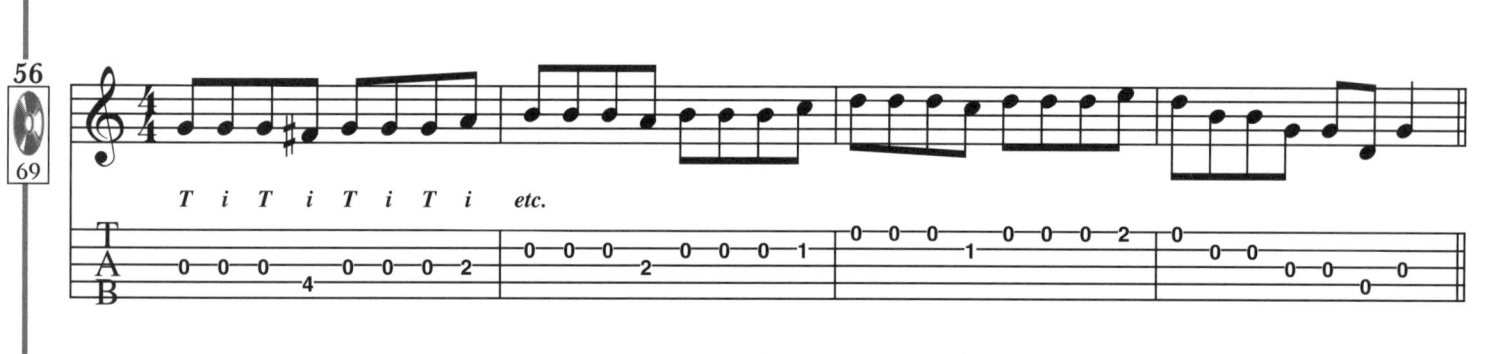

Players who want to incorporate classical music or jazz and swing in their five-string banjo repertoire (think Béla Fleck) often use single-string playing. Below is an A Harmonic Minor scale that you will use to play the following swing-style lead break. The harmonic minor scale features a lowered 3rd and 6th degree (♭3 and ♭6). This gives it an exotic, Middle-Eastern sound.

A HARMONIC MINOR SCALE

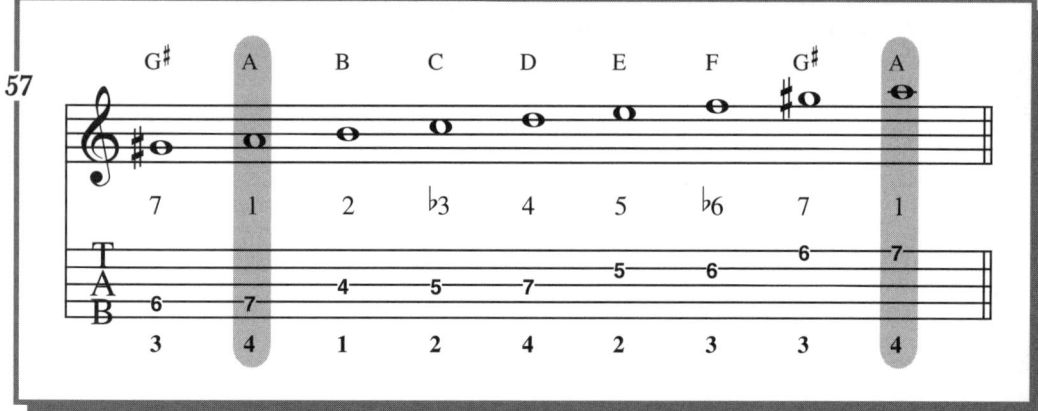

Now try your single-string chops on this short solo over a progression in A Minor. Chords have been included so that you can try your own improvisations using the A Harmonic Minor scale. Also, notice the "*Swing 8ths*" indication. See page 22 for information about swing 8ths.

MELODIC BANJO

This style was pioneered by Bill Keith in the 1960s and quickly became a staple among five-string players. The melodic style exploits the tuning of the five-string banjo, which has a higher-numbered string (the 5th string) that is higher in pitch than lower-numbered strings. This is called a *re-entrant* tuning. Re-entrant tunings allow intricate melodies to be played easily using separate strings for each note. Guitarists and mandolinists call this technique *cross-string picking*.

The melodic sound involves some very creative fingering to avoid playing two consecutive notes on the same string. The benefit is that the melody notes sustain through each other, creating a harp-like effect. The banjo has virtually no sustain even in the best of circumstances, so every little bit helps!

The Multi-Instrumental Guitarist • 63

Here are some G Major scale fingerings in the melodic style. Note that as you work up the fingerboard, the scale breaks up into four- or five-note fragments that often overlap. This allows more possibilities for fingerings to accommodate your melodies.

G MAJOR SCALE (MELODIC BANJO)

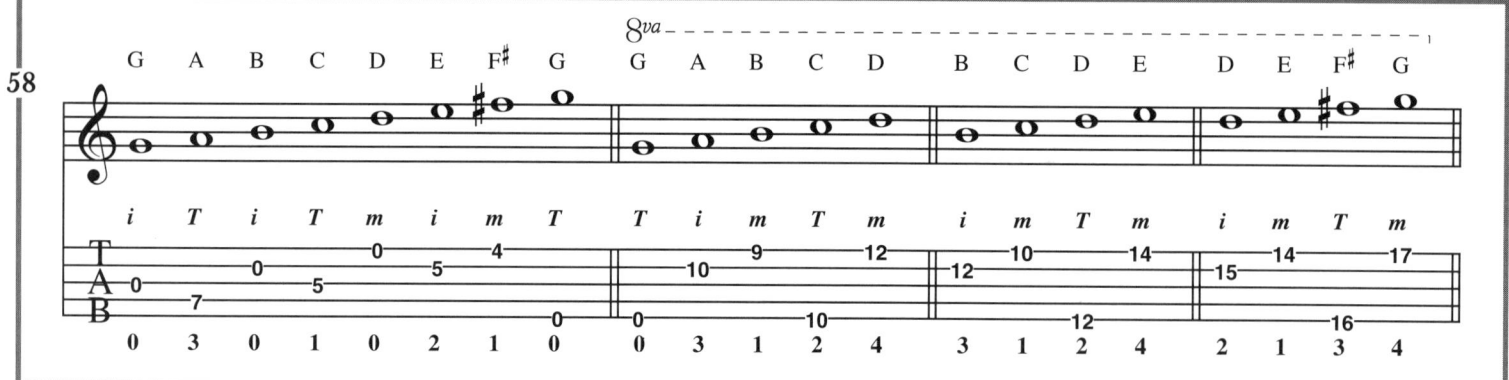

The melodic style is excellent for playing intricate Irish and American fiddle tunes. When played in the rolling style, some of the notes and character of the melodies get blurred out by bluesy banjo licks. The melodic style allows players to authentically reproduce the true melodies of the tunes. Here is a version of the Shaker melody "Simple Gifts," which is easily played using the 1st and 3rd finger of the left hand in the area of the *5th position* (around the 5th fret).

SIMPLE GIFTS (LOW OCTAVE)

64 • The Multi-Instrumental Guitarist

Now try "Simple Gifts" in the higher register of the banjo. Watch the finger placements very carefully. You will be fretting the 5th string to get some of your notes. Try to hold your fingers down on each note as long as possible, so that each string rings until the finger absolutely must be changed to play a new note on that string.

ROCK 'N' ROLL BANJO

The five-string banjo has found its way into many styles of rock music. Earl Scruggs himself formed a rock band in the 1970s with his sons called the Earl Scruggs Review. Neil Young, R.E.M., the Pogues, the Violent Femmes, Wilco and many others have employed the funky drive of the banjo over the years.

Rock and roll banjo allows for the incorporation of all the sounds you have used so far, as well as the discovery of new ones. To get you started, here are a couple of versions of "The Ballad of Excelsior Jones," also seen in the section on "Rock 'n' Roll Mandolin." This chord progression uses some minor chords and suspensions that are more common in rock than in traditional bluegrass.

The first version uses a rolling sound with some slides, bends, hammer-ons and pull-offs. This is somewhat reminiscent of the style heard on Neil Young's "Old Man" and Tony Trishka's playing on the Violent Femmes "Country Death Song."

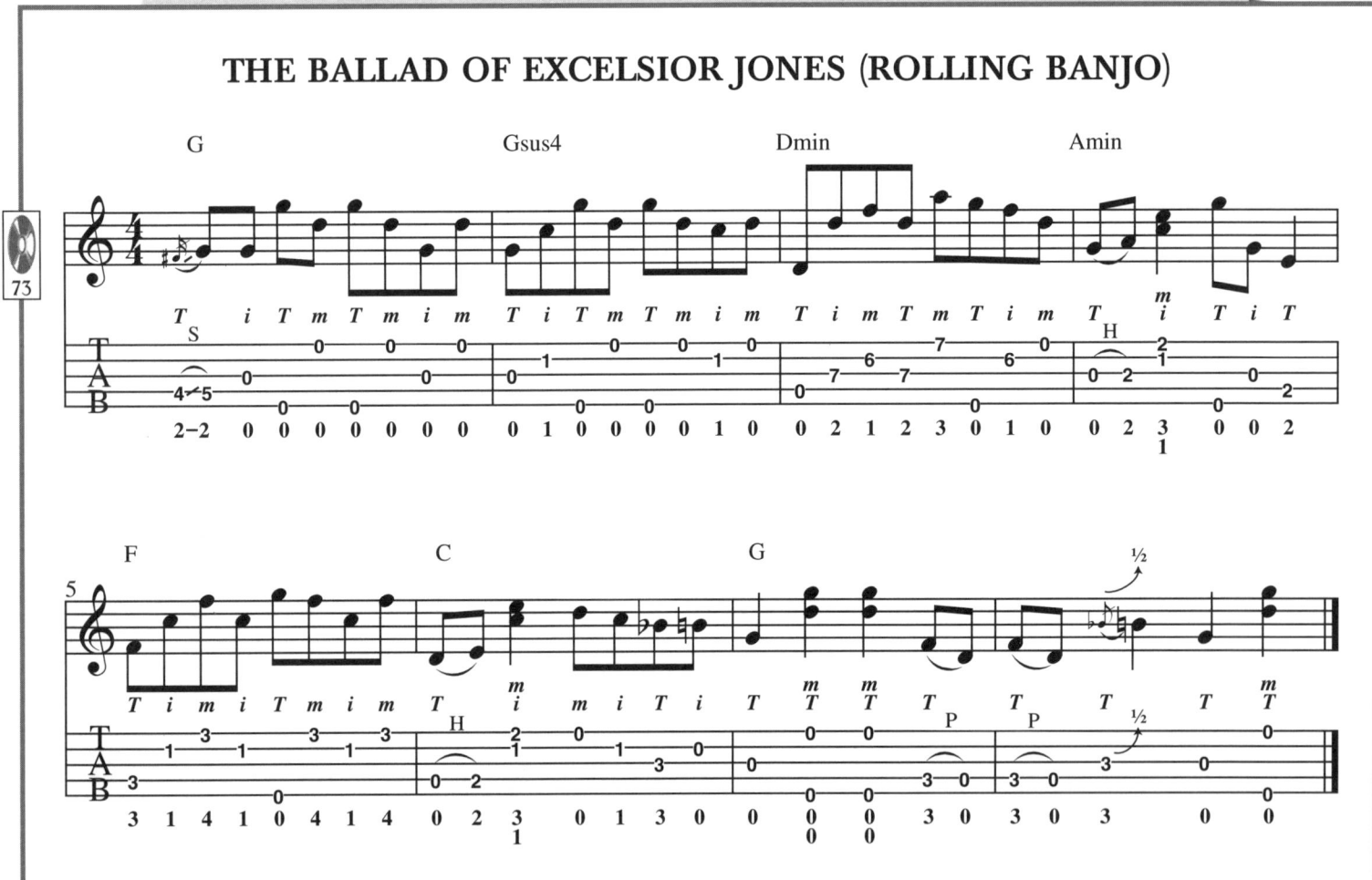

66 • The Multi-Instrumental Guitarist

Now try this version, which incorporates some blues and melodic licks for a more "lead banjo" or solo sound. Note the fretting of the 5th string in measures 6 and 7. Be sure to follow the finger placements exactly to avoid getting tripped up; recent cutbacks in the medical insurance industry have radically driven up the price of emergency *banjo-philangeal pretzelitis* ("pretzel-fingers") surgery.

THE BALLAD OF EXCELSIOR JONES (MELODIC BANJO)

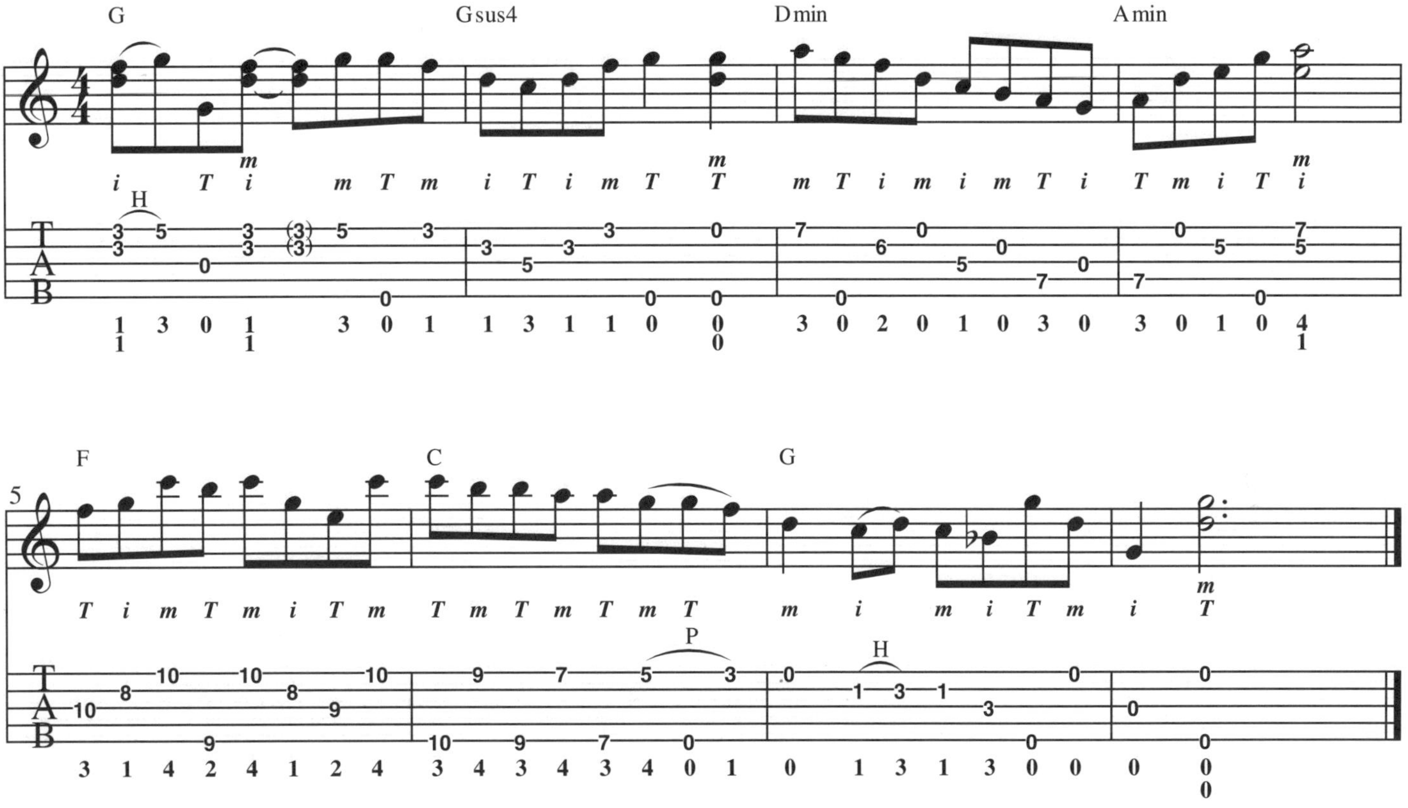

Tony Trischka has helped to redefine the banjo, its technical vocabulary and the contexts in which it is heard. To date he has recorded 12 solo albums featuring artists such as David Grisman, Pete Seeger, Béla Fleck, Jerry Douglas, William S. Burroughs, Charles Osgood, Alison Krauss, the Violent Femmes and members of R.E.M. Tony's musical travels have taken him from Broadway to Croatia to New Zealand, and he has performed with bluegrass bands, avant-garde jazz groups, symphony orchestras and percussion ensembles. He has appeared on the radio shows *A Prairie Home Companion, Mountain Stage, Fresh Air* and *Weekend Edition,* performed with John Denver on the CBS Hallmark Hall of Fame *production* Foxfire, *starring Hume Cronyn and Jessica Tandy, and was profiled, along with Béla Fleck, on CBS News Sunday Morning. Tony is also the author of* Banjo for Beginners, *also published by the National Guitar Workshop and Alfred.*

CHAPTER 7
UKULELE

If the banjo is happy, then the *ukulele* is positively euphoric. It was introduced to Hawaii as a tiny travel guitar in the hands of Portuguese sailors. Given its name by the Hawaiians, which means "leaping flea," the ukulele is as much a state of mind as an instrument; it seems to communicate nothing but fun and childlike wonder.

The ukulele has held a giggling corner in the tea party of music history since the 1920s and its feature performers range from early American jazz-age star "Ukulele Ike," to British music hall performers such as George Formby, to modern revivalists Tiny Tim, Ian Whitcomb and Jim Beloff. Even the Who recorded a song with the uke on their album *Who By Numbers*. Ukuleles are also found in a banjo version, called a *banjo-uke* or a *banjolele*. The leaping flea has proven easy to catch, pleasing to scratch, and hard to shake off.

If you are planning to acquire a ukulele, make sure that it has working tuners! Most ukes have friction pegs (they don't have gears like guitar tuners), and these can wear out and slip. Also make sure the neck is fretted well and plays reasonably in tune. The combination of thick nylon strings and the tiny scale length mean that most ukes will never be perfectly in tune. Some refer to this as "charm."

Soprano Ukulele

Ukuleles have four strings, often nylon. Like many instruments that blossomed in the 1920s, the uke can be found in many sizes, tunings and pitch ranges. This chapter will focus on the *soprano uke* (the common "tiny guitar" ukulele). The next chapter will provide some information on the larger *baritone uke*.

UKULELE TUNING

The soprano ukulele is tuned to a C6 chord (G–C–E–A). This tuning mimics the arrangement of intervals on the first four strings of standard guitar tuning, transposed up a 4th. Imagine your guitar capoed at the 5th fret, missing the 5th and 6th strings. Then imagine that the 4th string is actually tuned up an octave. Thus is the tuning of the ukulele. This tuning, when strummed from the 4th string to the 1st, sounds the melody known as "My Dog Has Fleas." Here are the open strings and matching frets.

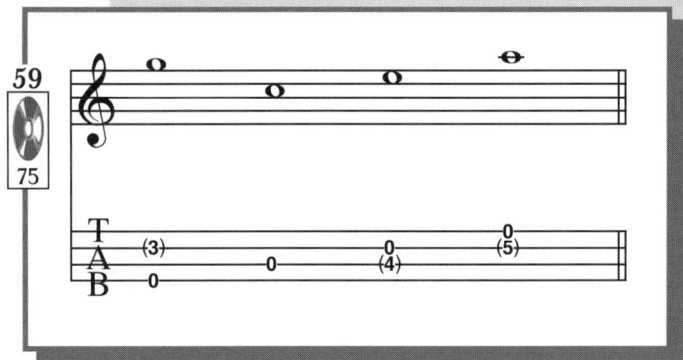

Banjo Ukulele

OPEN CHORDS

Ukulele chord shapes are just like guitar shapes, but you will have to relearn which chord is which because of the tuning. The small size and close position of the frets also suggests a different approach to fingering than the guitar. Here are some basic chords for the uke.

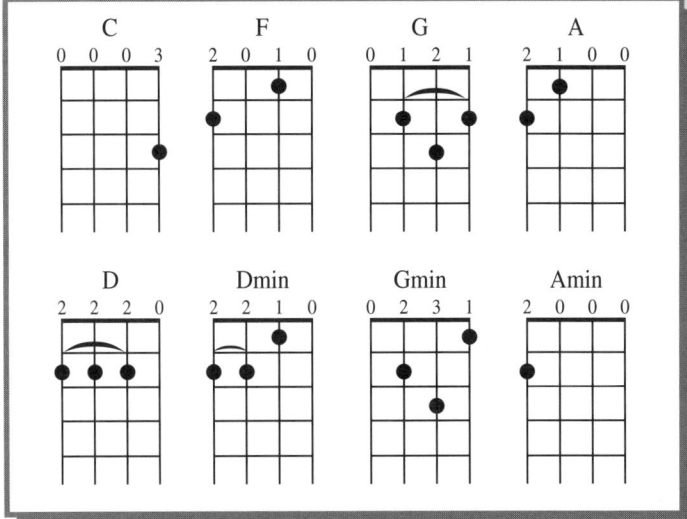

MOVABLE CHORDS

These chord shapes resemble some of the barre chord positions you have learned on the guitar, with a few new possibilities.

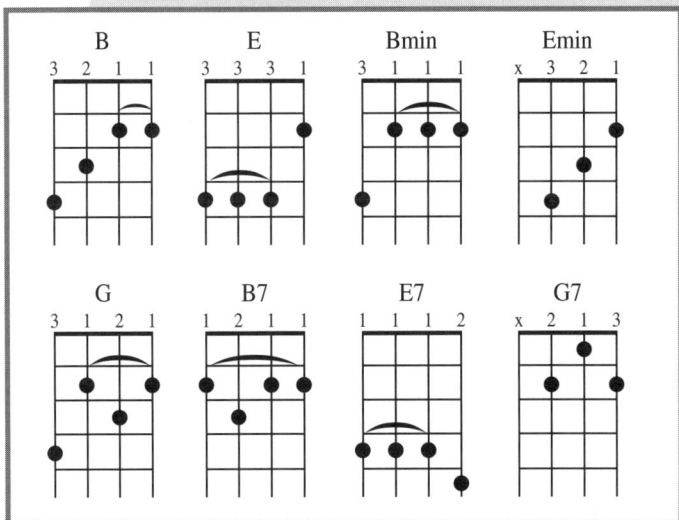

STRUMMING

While the sweet plunk of lead uke is intriguing, the ukulele is best known as a strumming instrument. Traditional players often strum back and forth with the index finger or thumb; other players use a pick. You can also use a pick made of thick felt, specially designed for ukulele strumming.

The common strum for the 1920s pop songs is a basic one. You can remember it with the phrase "dum-diddy-dum-diddy." Try this example.

Basic "Dum-Diddy" Strum

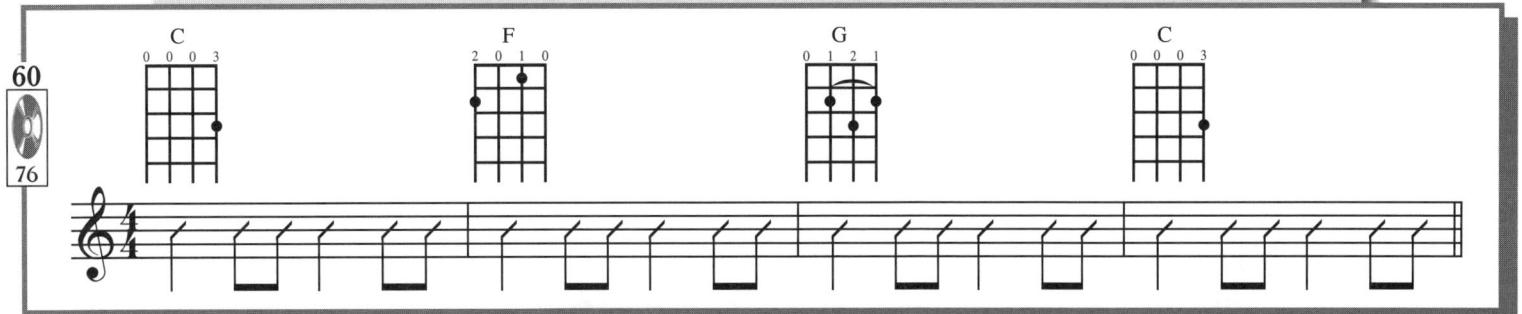

OLD TIME BANJO UKE

The banjo uke has become very popular in old-time fiddle jams. Jeff Klaus of the old-time/jungle throb fusion band the Horseflies uses banjo uke to drive fiddle tunes and for minimalist rhythmic explorations. His strum involves steady eighth notes with accents on beats 2 and 4. Think "wakachicka-wakachicka." Try the chords to "Soldier's Joy" with this strum, then try playing along with the mandolin version on page 19 (track 8 on the CD). Of course, this strum will work on a soprano uke, too.

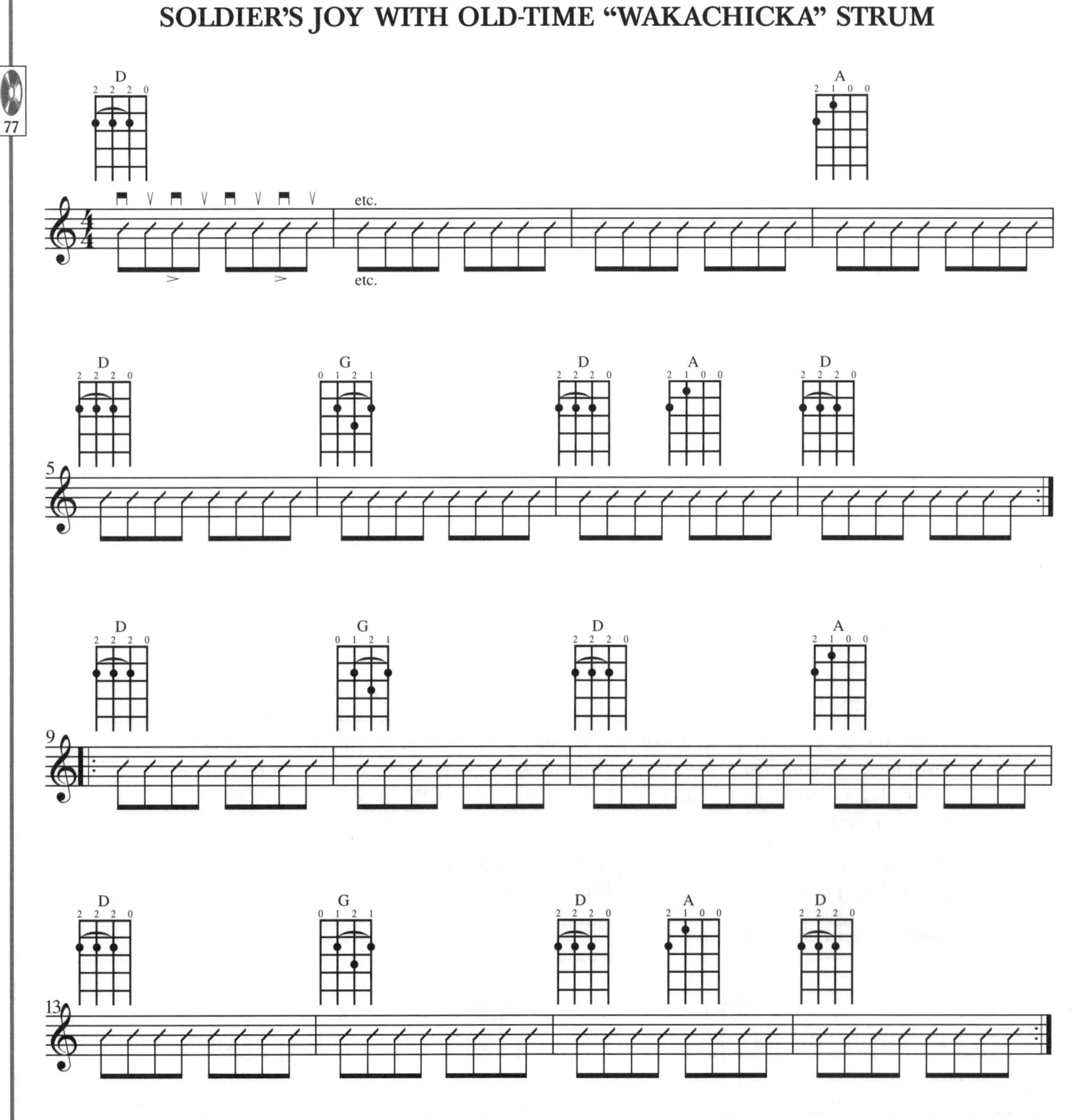

70 • The Multi-Instrumental Guitarist

ADVANCED UKE

The more colorful ukulele performers use lots of chord voicings and rhythmic flourishes to spice up the music. Some even use special effects like *tremolo* (strumming back and forth rapidly) or tossing the instrument around like a juggler. With the use of some rhythmic variety and using chord voicings up and down the fingerboard, it is possible to give melodic direction to your chord strumming. Try "Ukehula Boogaloola" to get an idea of the possibilities. Note the use of *passing chords* (a harmony from outside the key that is placed between two chords from within the key, usually found on weak beats) including augmented chords. An easy trick, which gives a sense of motion, is to move your chords up or down one half step, then back to the intended chord. Standard music notation has been included so you can see the melody implied by the high notes of the chords. No TAB is given because all of the notes used are shown in the chord diagrams above the music.

CHAPTER 8
BARITONE UKE AND TENOR GUITAR (GUITAR TUNING)

This short chapter is devoted to two instruments you already know how to play. *Baritone Ukes* look like shrunken, four-string guitars; some have steel-strings, others have nylon strings. The baritone uke is tuned the same as the first four strings of the standard guitar. This tuning is also a popular variation for tenor guitars and banjos. In the 1920s and '30s, instrument makers were churning out simple, inexpensive, portable strumming instruments in all sizes for the masses. The baritone uke coule easily be mastered by ukulele players, guitar players and just about everyone else. It had a lower range than the uke, making it a more mellow and pleasing sound.

BARITONE UKE AND TENOR GUITAR TUNING
Here are the open strings and matching frets for this tuning.

OPEN CHORDS
Guitarists will recognize these right away.

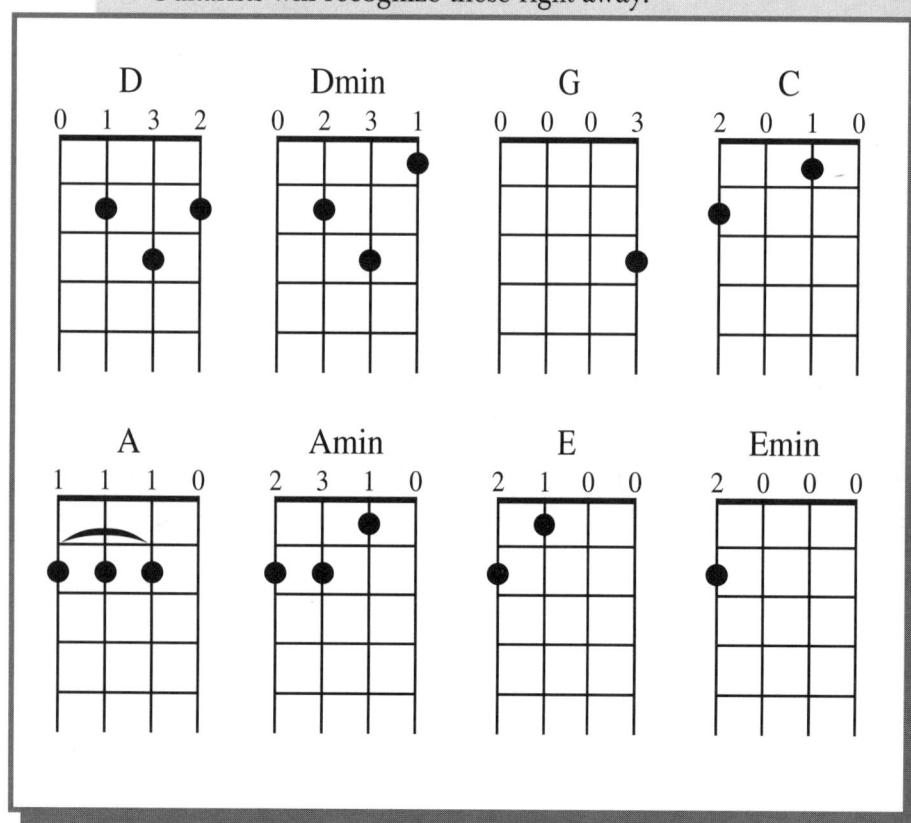

MOVABLE CHORDS

These are identical to guitar and ukulele chords. Depending on the length of the neck on your baritone uke or tenor guitar, you may wish to adjust the fingerings to make them more comfortable.

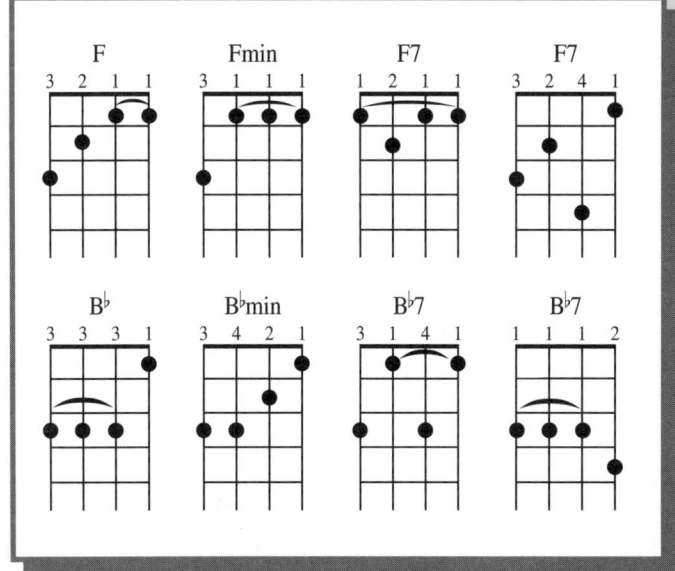

Here's a little tune to try in the "stand-in-the-yard-at-midnight-and-throw-a-pebble-at-your-lover's-window-then-serendade-him/her-with-sweet-strums-and-tremulous-vocalizations" style. Try strumming quarter notes with your thumb for the rhythm part; then try the melody.

(NO BETTER SWEATER THAN) LAURA'S ANGORA

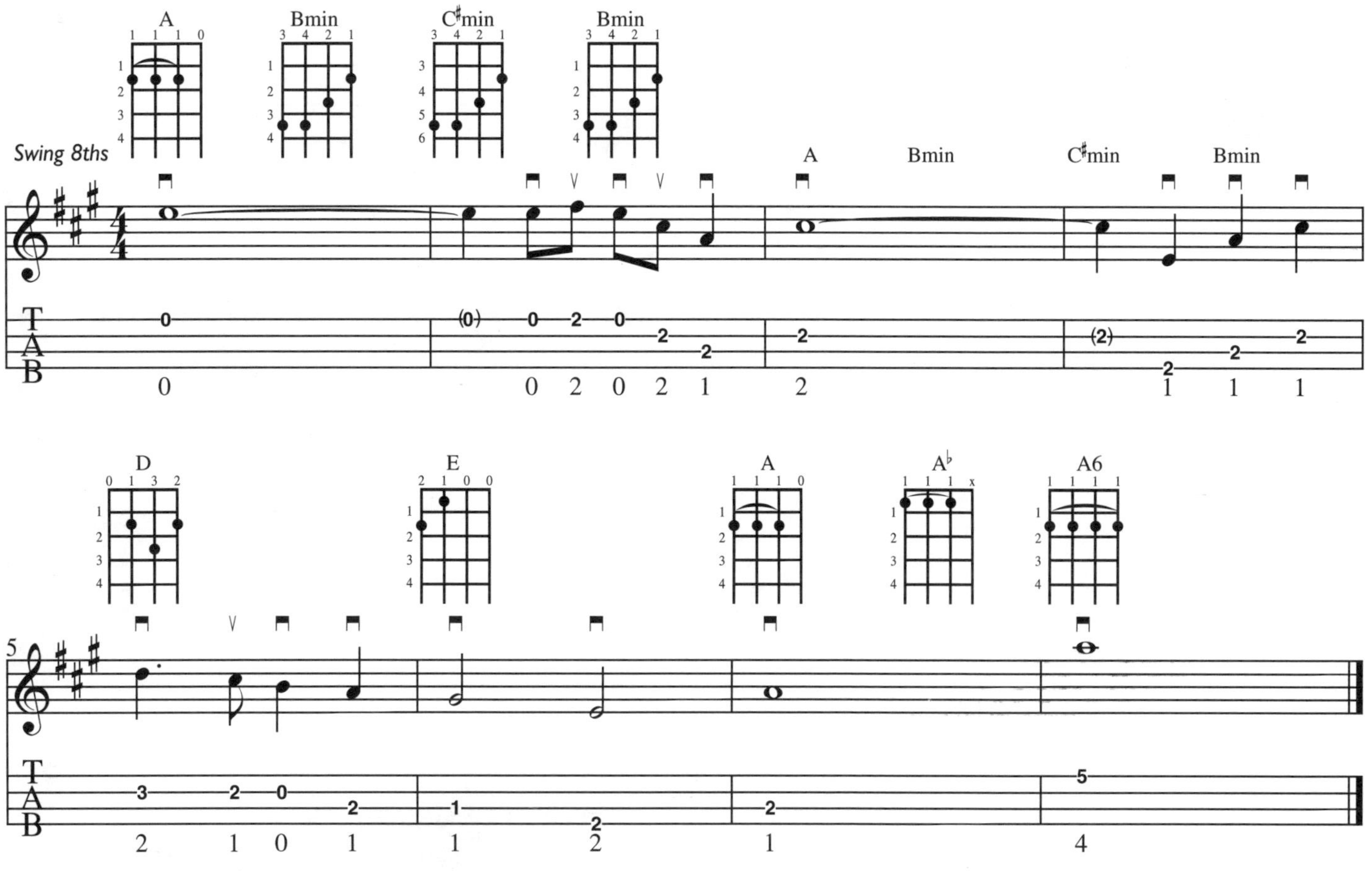

CHAPTER 9
LAP DULCIMER

The *lap dulcimer* is also known as the *Appalachian dulcimer* or *mountain dulcimer*. It is basically a fretboard with three or four strings and a teardrop- or hourglass-shaped sound chamber, held in the lap and strummed. This instrument is not to be confused with the *hammered dulcimer*, which has many strings, no frets and is played by striking the strings with small wooden "hammers."

Traditional dulcimer playing is rooted in the Appalachian mountains. The melody is played without chords against two open drone strings, giving a sound similar to bagpipe music (only much quieter). In modern times, many enterprising musicians, including Joni Mitchell, Richard Thompson, and Peter Buck of R.E.M. incorporated it into rock music.

The best thing about the dulcimer is that you already know how to play it. Congratulations, another one for the résumé! But seriously, this is one of the simplest fretted instruments ever designed. Just place it in your lap with the tuners to the left and the "scoop" or "strumming hollow" (dip in the fretboard) to your right.

MIXOLYDIAN TUNING AND THE MIXOLYDIAN MODE

Most dulcimers have three or four strings. If you have three strings, the melody is fretted on the string closest to your belly, the other two are left open as drones. If you have four strings, the two closest to you are set closer together than the others. These are tuned identically and fretted together, making the melody sound louder than on a three-string dulcimer.

The tablature follows the traditional dulcimer format which places the melody string (or strings) on the bottom line and the drones above. There are a several common tunings. In this book, we will use what is often called *Mixolydian tuning*: D–A–D. Notice that the dulcimer sounds in the same octave it is written.

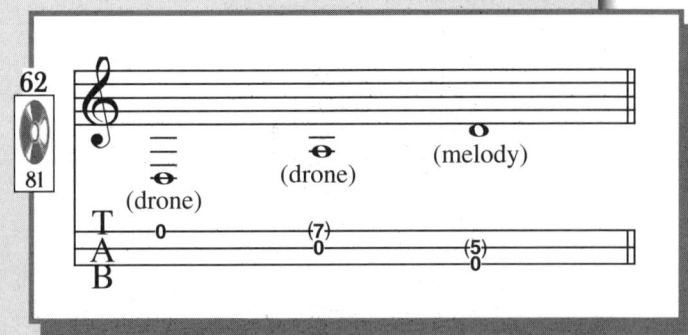

The lap dulcimer frets form the Mixolydian mode. In other words, the frets on the dulcimer only sound a D Major scale with a lowered 7th degree (♭7); it has a C-natural instead of a C-sharp. This is why the frets appear at uneven intervals along the board. There are six frets in the scale; the 7th fret begins the next octave.

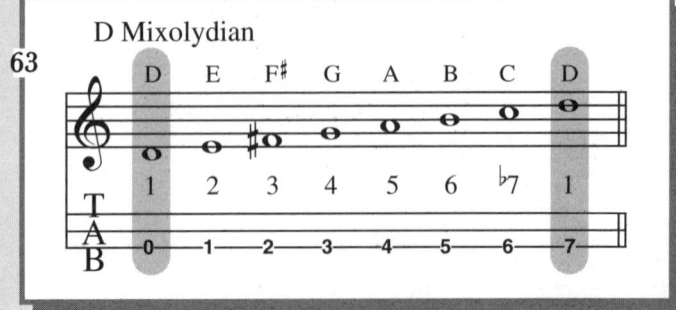

> **NOTE:**
> Some modern dulcimers include an extra fret for the natural 7th degree of the major scale. Since the Mixolydian mode uses six frets, dulcimer players and teachers refer to this extra fret as the "6th-and-a-half fret." Accept it and move on! This book does not require the 6½ fret, so skip over it if you have one.

FRETTIN' AND STRUMMIN'

You only need one finger to fret the dulcimer in the traditional style, though you may use more. Many players use a *noter* to fret the melody string instead of the fingers. A noter is a small piece of wood, like a dowel stick or popsicle stick, held between the thumb and index finger of the left hand. Using a noter or one finger causes the slippery, sitar-like sliding from note to note that is the trademark of traditional dulcimer style.

Below is a traditional fiddle tune heard at many jams and festivals. It is in the Mixolydian mode and sounds great on the dulcimer. Strum all the strings as indicated in the TAB. Note that the music notation only shows the melody, so that you can more clearly see the shape of the tune.

Notice that the downstrum sign ⊓ now indicates a strum away from you; the upstrum sign V indicates a strum towards yourself. If your "upstrums" don't always catch the melody string, that's okay. Playing the lap dulcimer, and notating its music, is far from an exact science. This is mountain music; relax and have fun.

⊓ = Strum away from yourself
V = Strum toward from yourself

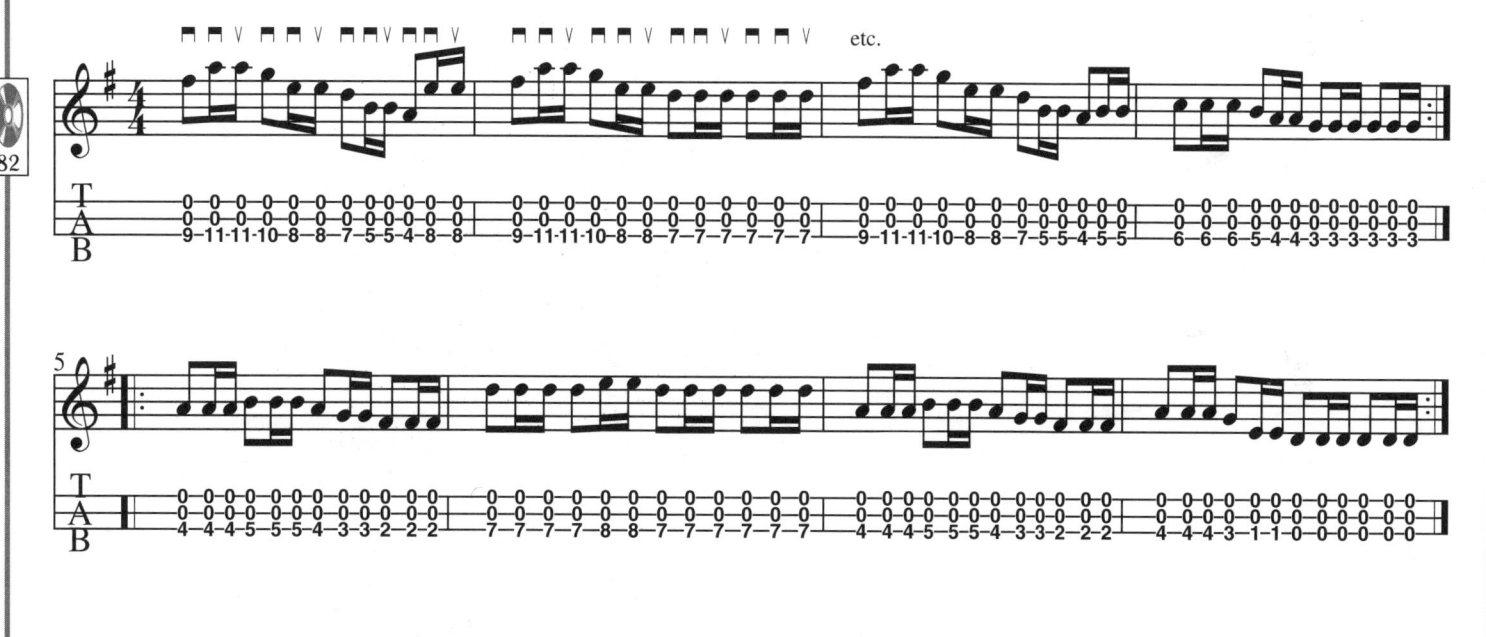

DULCIMER AS A MODAL INSTRUMENT

The cool thing about the dulcimer's fret arrangement is that it allows you to play in different modal scales without learning new fingerings. For example, try playing the scale on the middle string (the "A" string). The tonic note of D is on the 3rd fret. Now you have a D Major scale with a natural 7th degree (C#).

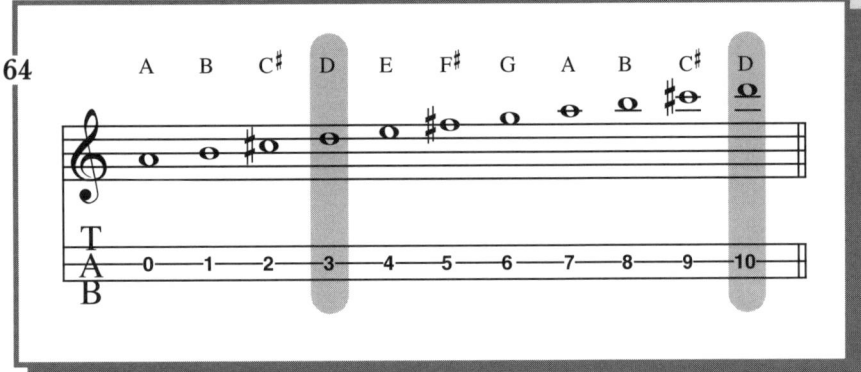

Try this traditional old-time tune using the middle string as the melody (fret with your finger so that you can use the other strings as drones).

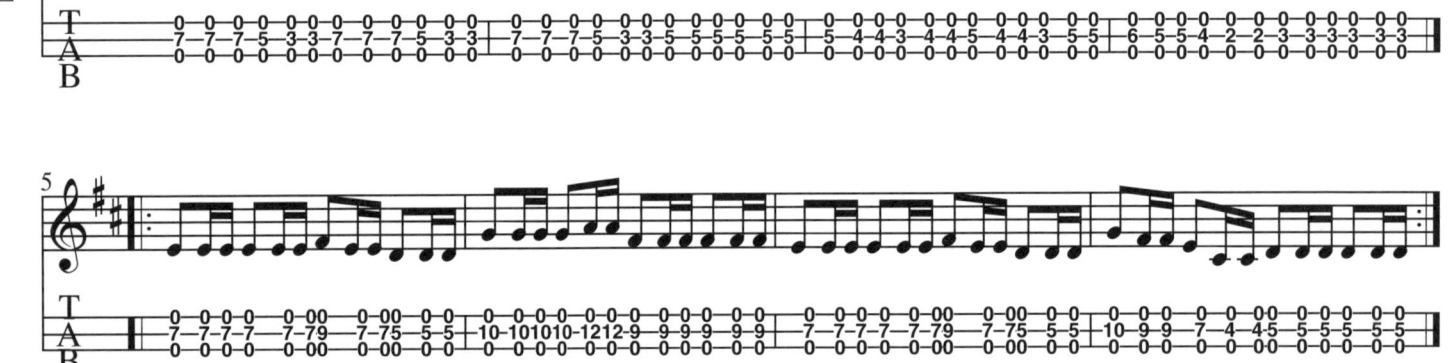

NOTE:
To take full advantage of this new version of the scale, dulcimer players use the D–A–A or *Ionian mode tuning*. Tune the melody strings down to A, and play the scale on the melody strings. This gives a D Major, or D Ionian, scale starting on the 3rd fret, now on the melody strings (example 64, above, shows the scale on the middle string).

ADVANCED DULCIMER PLAYING

The more progressive modern dulcimer players fret notes on the drone strings to make chords and harmonies for the melodies. Some even use a fingerstyle picking approach to broaden the possibilities. Here is "Rock That Cradle, Joe" with the melody on the D string and harmony notes on the A string. All you have to do is follow one fret above the melody!

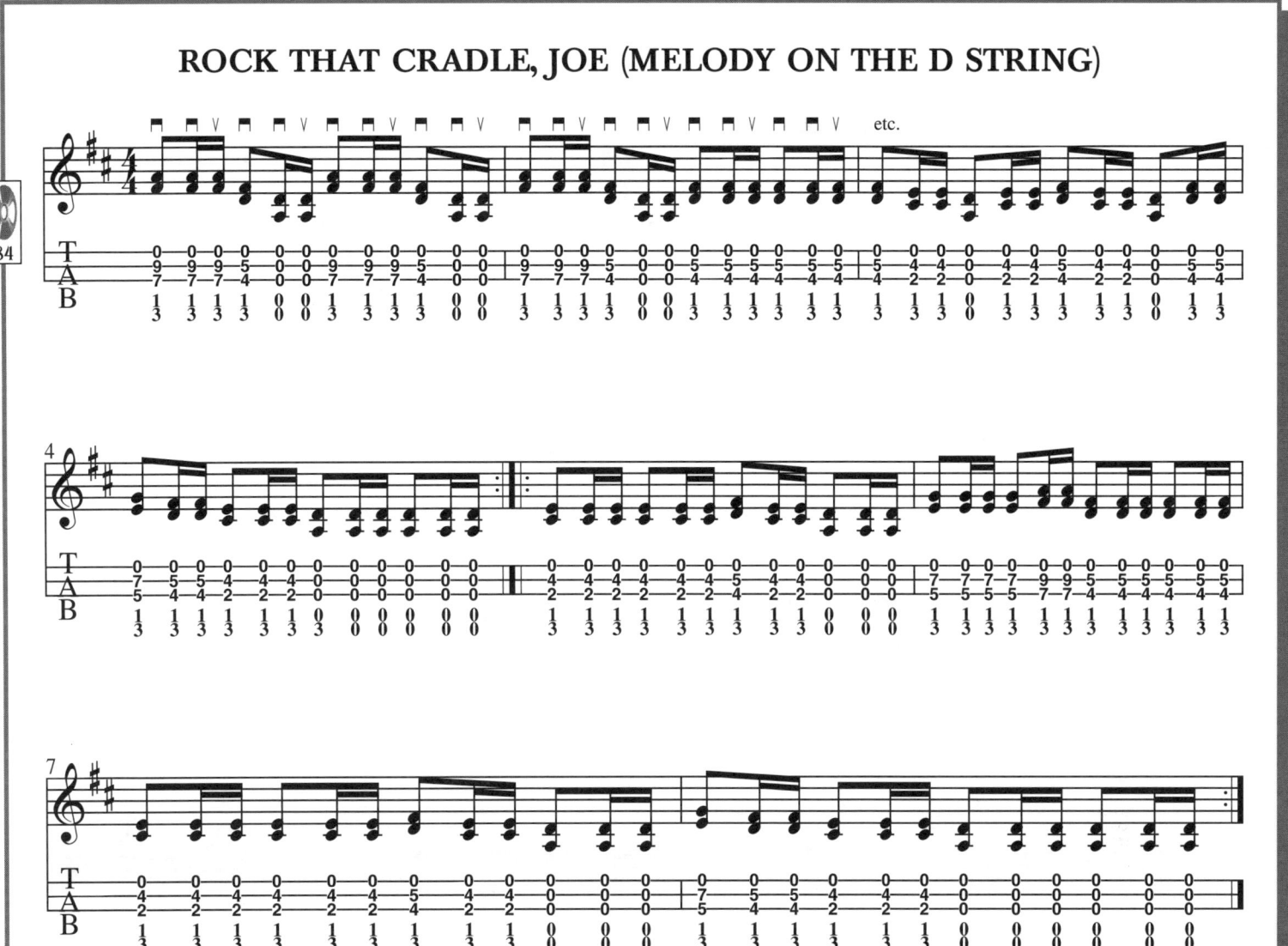

CHAPTER 10
LAP SLIDE GUITAR

Using a slide makes playing *lap slide guitar* very different than playing a standard guitar. Before digging in, let's review some of the types of slide guitars that are out there, talk a bit about tuning and strings, and then some basic slide technique.

TYPES OF SLIDE GUITARS

Lap slide guitar is otherwise known as *steel guitar*. The style was developed in Hawaii in the late nineteenth century, and so was originally called *Hawaiian guitar*. Nowadays this term usually refers to lap slide played in the style specific to the Hawaiian Islands. Dobro® is a copyrighted name (owned by the Gibson company) that is incorrectly used in a generic way to describe lap slide guitars. It actually refers to a particular brand of the most common type of lap slide, an acoustic *resonator* guitar. There are many skilled luthiers currently making excellent lap resonator guitars.

Then there is the *lap steel* or *table steel*. These usually refer to solid body, electric, square-neck guitars. The latter often have multiple necks and are mounted on legs. *Pedal steel* refers to a table steel with pedals and knee levers that can change the pitch of the strings without having to move the slide bar.

You can use any standard guitar to play lap style. Many players use a *nut raiser* to elevate the strings so that the slide bar does not come in contact with the guitar neck. These are inexpensive devices but you will probably have to special order one at a music store. The strings are raised approximately one half to three-quarters of an inch above the fretboard for added distance to help avoid the bar striking the neck. Raising the strings, however, increases tension and with that comes the possibility of warping the neck. Don't do this on an expensive instrument without the guidance of an experienced luthier. Guitars made for lap playing usually have square necks for the strength needed to withstand the added pressure of raising the strings.

Resonator Guitar

Hawaiian Guitar

Double Neck Electric Guitar

G MAJOR TUNING (HIGH BASS G TUNING)

There are several tunings for lap steel playing in common use these days. We will concentrate on the most common: *high bass G tuning*. This tuning has the benefit of being similar to standard guitar tuning. Below is the tuning from the 6th (lowest) string to the 1st (highest). Notice that it forms two G Major triads (G–B–D). The matching notes on adjacent strings for tuning are included in parentheses.

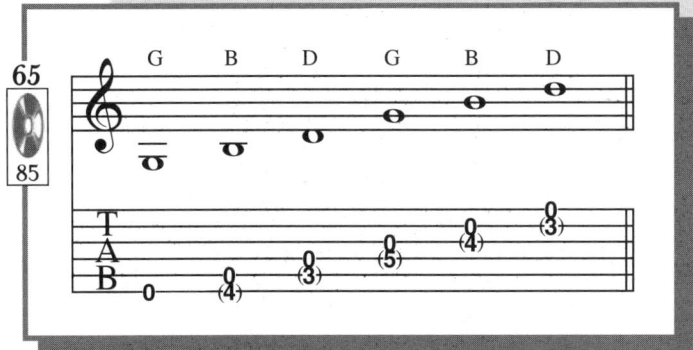

The 2nd, 3rd and 4th strings are tuned the same as in guitar standard tuning, but the 1st string is a whole step lower (D instead of E). Most solo work is done on those top four strings.

The New York Times has called **Jerry Douglas** (b. 1956) "matchless contemporary master" of the Dobro®. He has won five Grammy Awards, several Grammy Acknowledgments, and countless specialized awards. Though he got his start in bluegrass, he has made an impact in fields ranging from rock 'n' roll to jazz, from blues to Celtic, from mainstream country to contemporary classical. He has defined the sounds of many diverse recordings, having played on more than 1,000 albums, including discs released by Garth Brooks, Paul Simon, James Taylor, Reba McEntire and Ray Charles, to name just a few.

STRINGS FOR PLAYING LAP SLIDE

The lighter gauges typically used on the first three strings of a standard guitar deliver too weak a tone. Typical string gauges for lap steel playing fall in the following ranges:

String	Gauge Range
1st:	.016 – .018
2nd:	.018 – .020
3rd:	.026 – .029
4th:	.035 – .039
5th:	.045 – .049
6th:	.056 – .059

Electric steel guitars are usually strung with the lighter of the gauges suggested above. Depending on personal taste, most players favor either nickel or phosphor-bronze strings, with the former more common on electrics and the latter on acoustics. Experiment.

When you first put them on, you may hear a bit of a grating noise from the strings when sliding. This effect disappears after the winding is ground down a bit by about an hour's playing. There are ground wound strings that have this job done for you in manufacturing, but most people find that these have less life than standard wound strings.

THE RIGHT HAND

Except for occasional solo playing, all lap slide guitarists use fingerpicks; usually metal ones on the index and middle fingers (although some players favor plastic fingerpicks) and a plastic thumbpick. Fingerpicks are necessary not only for volume, but because the high tension of the strings is rough on bare fingers and fingernails.

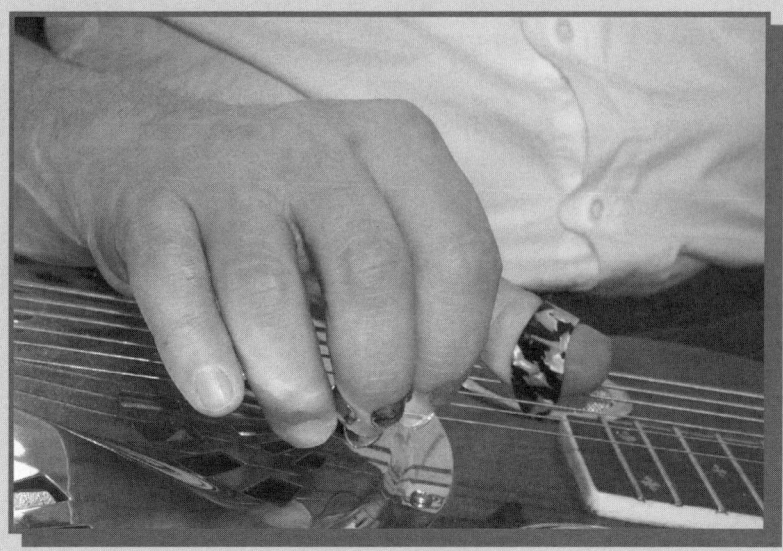

BARS (SLIDES)

The most important difference between playing a standard guitar and lap slide guitar is in the fretting hand. A solid piece of metal called a *bar* or *slide* is used to change the vibrating length of the string (the shorter the vibrating length, the higher the pitch) instead of using fingers to press the strings against the frets. The heavier the bar you use the better the tone will be—though too heavy a bar will make it hard to move quickly. Hollow bottleneck tubes are much too lightweight and should not be used.

The two most popular bar shapes are: the *bullet bar*, which is cylindrical with rounded ends; the other—often called a *Stevens bar* after the most popular make—has grooves on the top (for the index finger) and sides (for the thumb and middle finger) and, occasionally, angled ends. When using a Stevens bar, the fingers may not stay in the side grooves if they are sufficiently relaxed. Instead, they help with *damping* the strings (see the photos below). Acoustic slide players, especially bluegrass buffs, favor Stevens-style bars. Electric lap steel players most often use bullet bars.

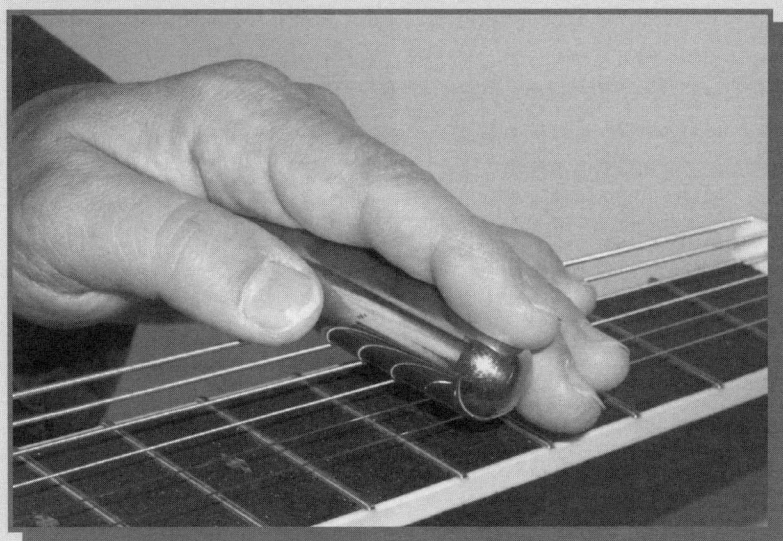

The Bullet Bar

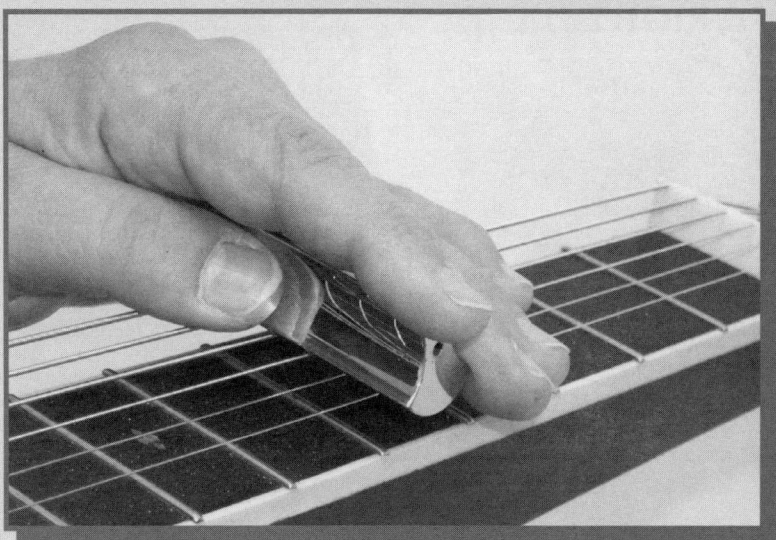

The Stevens Bar

BASIC LEFT-HAND TECHNIQUE

Fretting with a bar is like playing with one finger. So economy of motion should be a recurring mantra for students of slide guitar. The bar is laid gently on the strings without depressing them. The strings are never pressed all the way down to the fretboard. Let the weight of the bar do the work, holding it as loosely as possible. The fingers guide the bar, but do not squeeze it. Clutching tightly would slow you down and quickly tire your hand muscles. If, during the learning process, the bar occasionally slips out of your hand and falls to the floor, it is probably a good sign. During your first few months of using a bar, check your grip occasionally to avoid developing bad habits.

DAMPING

Lets try a D chord. Lay the bar flat, exactly over the 7th fret. You cannot rely on the frets to do the work for you, as on a standard guitar. As is playing the violin, your ears have to be constantly vigilant for questionable intonation. Since your sight line of the bar is at an angle, the bar may appear to be slightly behind the fret when it actually is directly over it. It should take only a short time to take this optical illusion into account. If you don't damp the strings before barring, you will fall victim to dreaded *bar chatter*—the rattling, metallic clatter of the bar and strings clanging together. Generally, your trailing fingers (those between the bar and nut) should touch the strings a split second before the bar hits the strings. If there still is some rattling, make sure that the bar lies absolutely flat on the strings (and that the strings lie on a flat plane). When the bar is lifted, the trailing fingers should remain on the strings, for at least a split second. Some players develop damping techniques using the picking hand, but for starters, left-hand damping is easiest, and very effective.

> **Note:** While some of the first generation of acoustic bottleneck players made chatter part of their sound, lap players tend to be fanatical about barring very cleanly. If you insist, you can always allow some rattle back into the sound after learning to damp effectively.

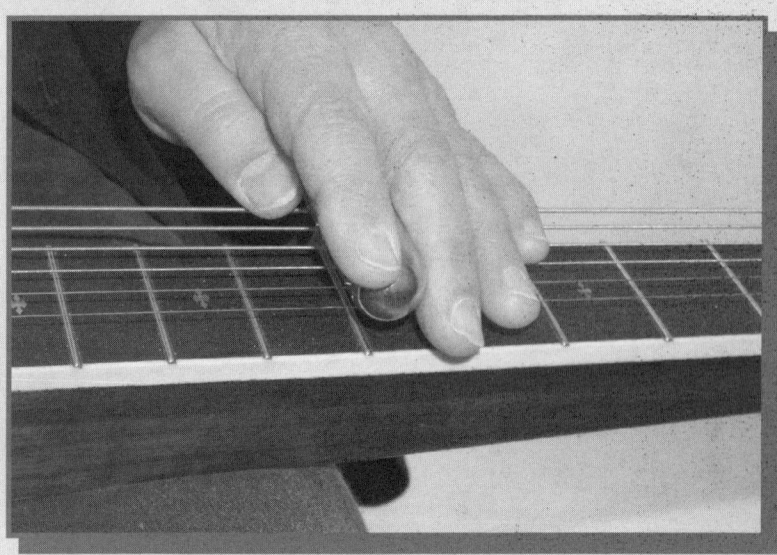

The bar should be directly over the fret. Notice that the trailing fingers are laid gently across the strings for use in damping.

PLAYING THE "STRUMMING BLUES IN D"

Try strumming the chords over a typical blues shuffle in the key of D (page 84). In an open G tuning, major chords are easy. You can play the single notes and strum multiple strings in the music below with the thumb (strumming from lowest-pitched string towards the highest) or play the single notes with the thumb and strum multiple strings with the index and/or middle fingers (moving from the highest-pitched string towards the lowest). The strums can catch as many strings as you wish—it is not necessary to play the exact strings shown in the standard music notation and TAB. Let's try for no slides–no gliding sounds—in this first tune. When you lift off the D chords on the 7th fret to play the open-string G chords, make sure the trailing fingers stay on the strings until after the bar is lifted. When you return to D, the trailing fingers precede the bar. Remember, the bar need be lifted only the tiniest fraction off of the strings to stop the sound. When you move from the 7th fret to the 2nd fret and back again, the bar should be lifted, but not the trailing, damping fingers.

Bob Brozman was born in New York in 1954 and has been involved in music since early childhood. A guitarist since age six, Bob discovered National guitars at age 13. In their unique sound, the young Bob found his musical calling. He studied music and ethnomusicology at Washington University, with an emphasis on the earliest roots of Delta blues. He has since also become a respected authority on historical Hawaiian music, publishing articles and amassing a large collection of 78 rpm records. He has produced five re-issue albums from this collection on the Rounder and Folklyric labels, documenting the best of Hawaiian music from 1915 to 1935. Bob has completed 13 full-length recordings.

STRUMMING BLUES IN D

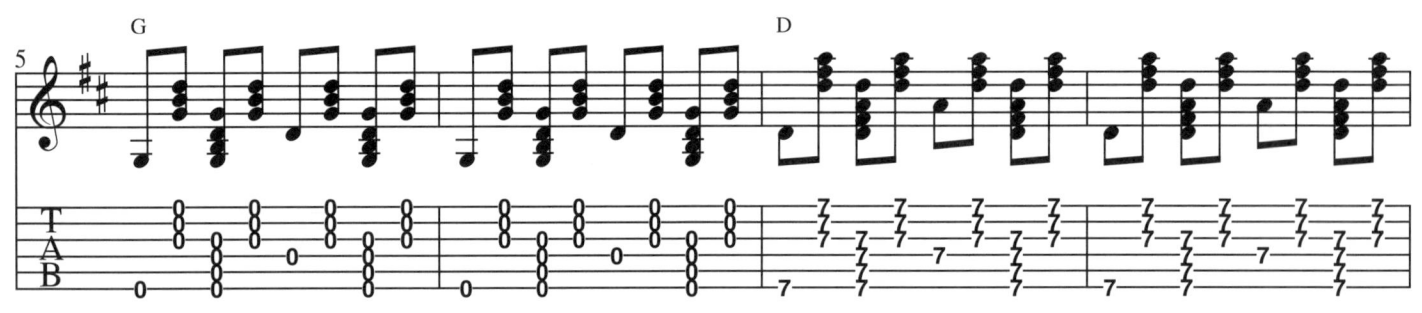
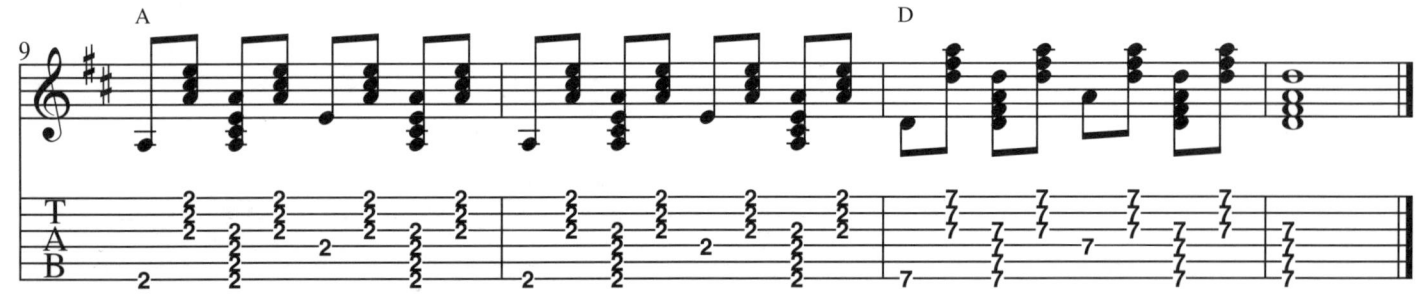

SINGLE-STRING TECHNIQUE AND SCALE PATTERNS

Let's tackle some single-string maneuvers. To avoid unnecessary chatter, the bar is tilted so that it touches only one string at a time. When tilting the bar, avoid the tendency to press down on the string, which would make the note sound sharp. Bend at the wrist instead of lifting the elbow or shoulder. Try the two-octave G Major scale shown below. Touch only the indicated strings with the tip of the bar. Damp between each note and perform no slides on this exercise. While slides are among the most pleasing effects of lap guitar, their over-use leads to the dreaded "Ha-whiney" guitar sound. Slide only when you want that sound, not by default or by accident. So, for now, slide only where indicated in the music notation.

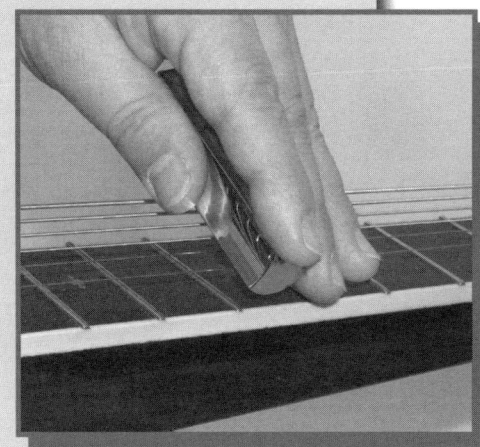

Tilting the bar

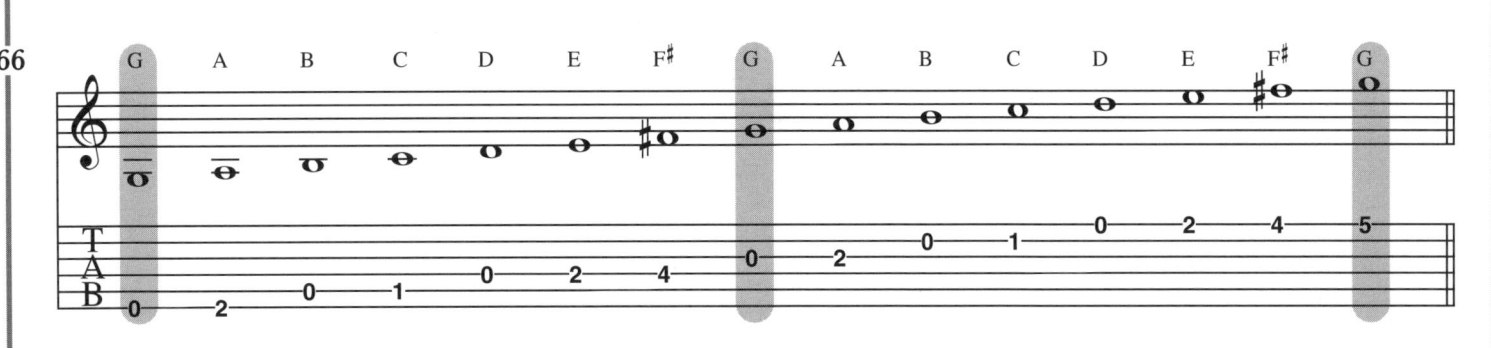

Below is the G Major scale again, but this time it is presented an octave higher. Since there are no open strings, the following patterns can be shifted up or down the neck to play any major scale. Two patterns are given; depending on the contour of the melody or lick, either might be preferable. Learn these patterns cold.

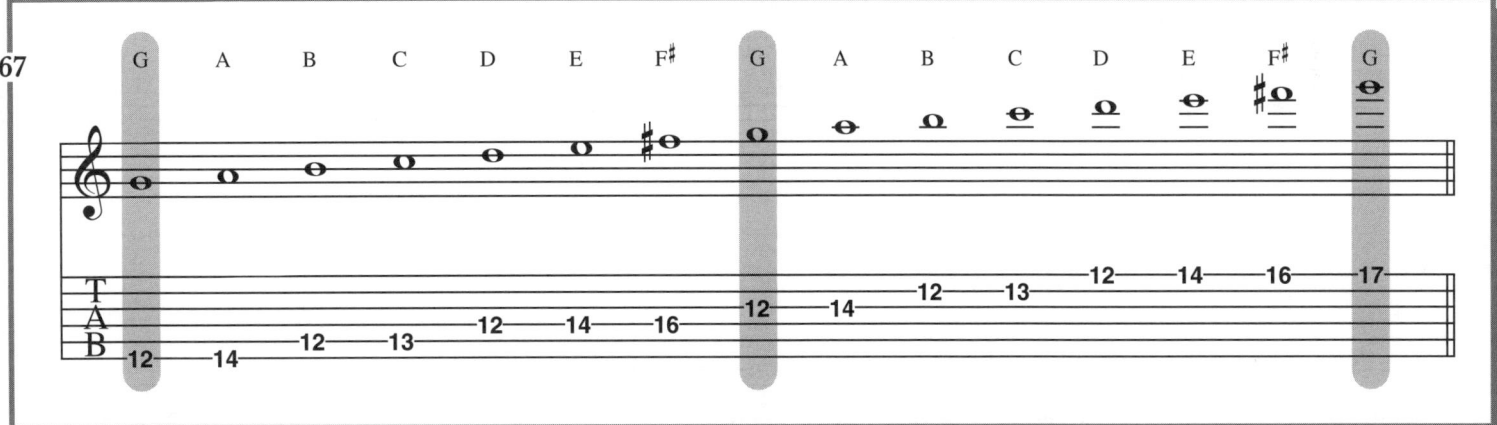

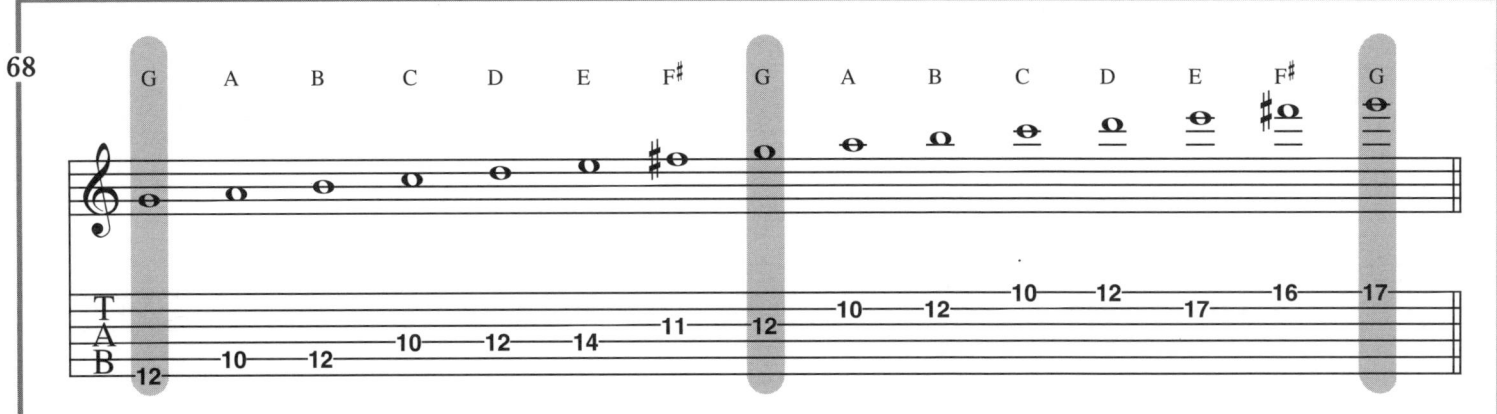

PLAYING "COUNTRY BLUES IN G"

Lets make some music! Play the following bluesy tune slowly, and as many times as necessary to eliminate all bar rattles. The notation is tricky to read because of the syncopation, so first listen to it on the CD. Check out the velocity and precision of the slides. While these *glissandi* are the most obvious move on lap guitar, being imprecise would make you sound sloppy. This is arranged to be played mostly on the 2nd, 3rd and 4th strings. These are tuned the same as standard guitar, so it should be easy to learn. The slow tempo of this piece allows for most any right-hand fingering, but the suggested pattern introduces your fingers to typical choices. Notes that are part of the accompanying chord need not be damped, because their sustain is consonant with the harmony. These notes include the open 3rd string that appears in several measures and the open 4th string in measure 14.

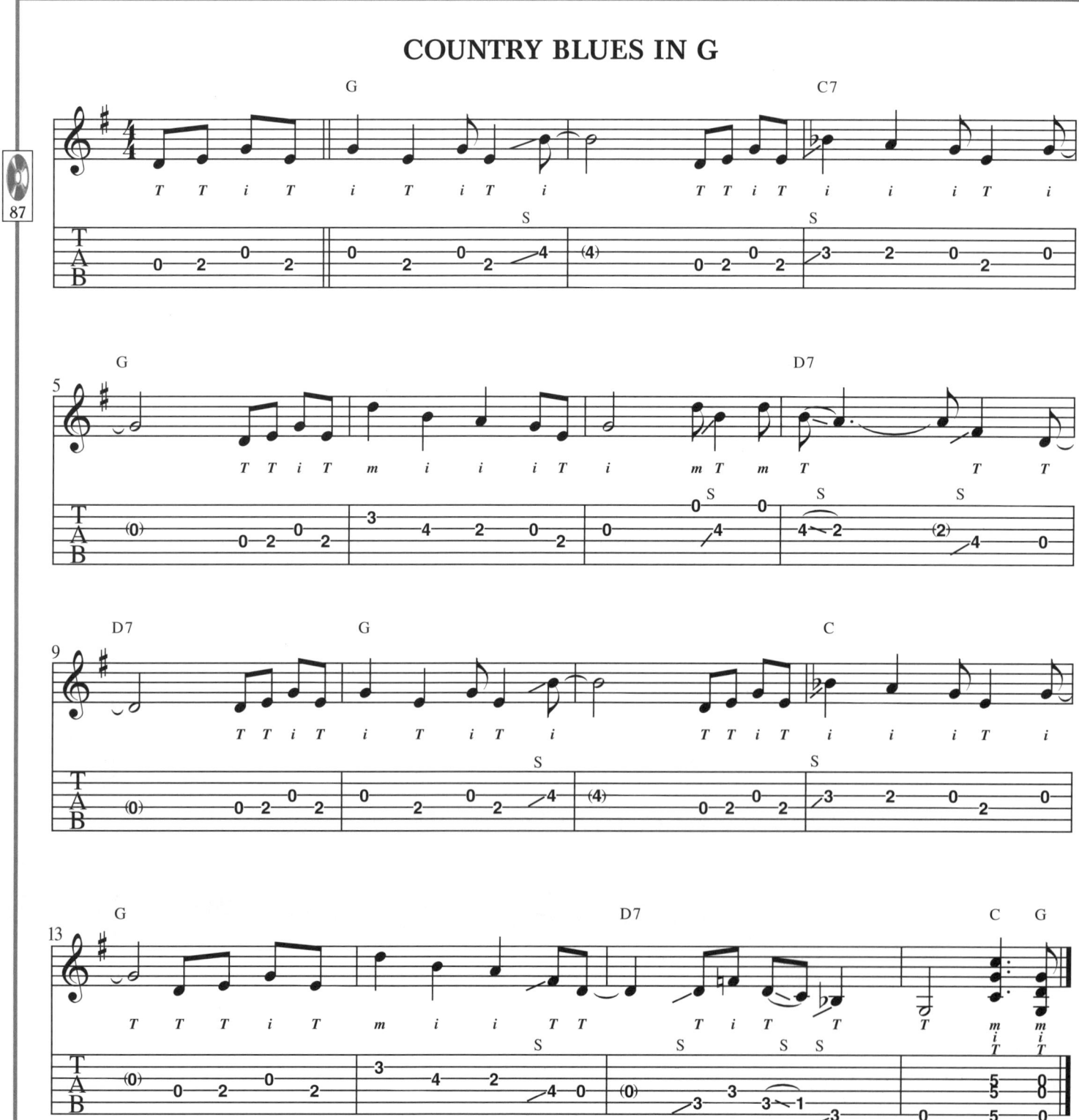

86 • The Multi-Instrumental Guitarist

DOUBLE STOPS AND VIBRATO

Double stops (two notes played simultaneously by one instrument) are some of the easiest and most pleasing lap slide techniques. Lap slide guitar was first developed in Hawaii, and the next piece has an Island feel that employs double stops. Again, concentrate on damping cleanly. The notes with an X above them are the most critical to damp. Make sure they sound for their entire duration, then lift the bar a fraction leaving your trailing fingers down on the strings, thus damping, and quickly move on to the next frets. Even at slow tempos, the moves between frets are usually fast. This avoids a *staccato* (short note) attack. Minimizing silences between notes when moving the bar is one of the most difficult techniques for beginners.

Most players would play all 1st and 2nd string figures with the index and middle fingers. You can do the same for 2nd- and 3rd-string double stops, or use the thumb and index finger or the thumb and middle finger. Experiment.

Add *vibrato* to any notes that last at least two beats. Vibrato is a rapid, vocal-like fluctuation of the pitch. There are a few ways to create vibrato with a bar. For now, try moving it back and forth smoothly around the target fret. Avoid jerky changes of direction; all motion should be from the wrist—do not move the forearm. Start the movement slowly, increasing the vibrating speed as the sound of the note decays. Usually, the width of vibration is about half the distance between frets, but this varies depending on the player and genre of music.

Junior Brown *was born in 1953 and raised in Kirksville, IN. With the help of guitar maker Michael Stevens, in 1985 he developed the "guit-steel," a double-necked guitar combining the standard guitar with the steel guitar. He made his album debut in 1993 with* 12 Shades of Brown, *which featured a tribute to his biggest influence, "My Baby Don't Dance to Nothing but Ernest Tubb."*

X = Dampen this note

DOUBLE STOP PIECE

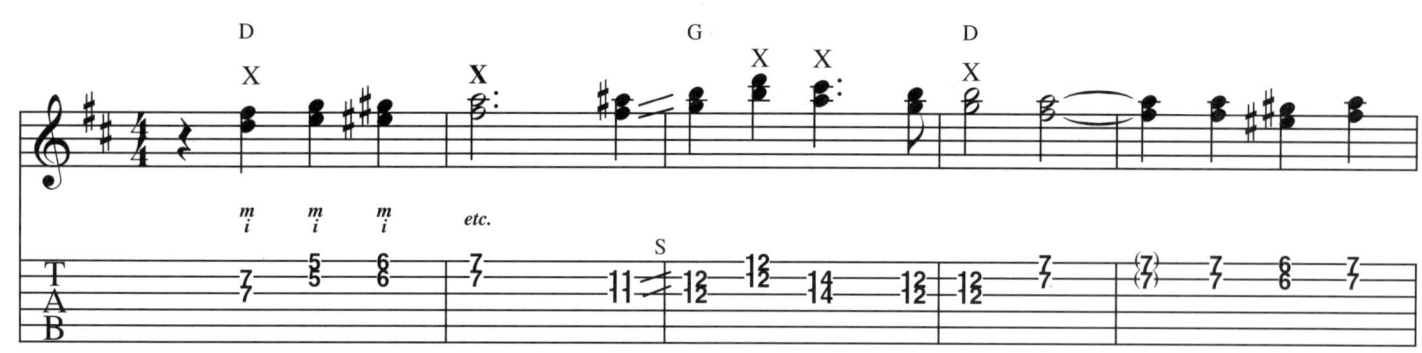

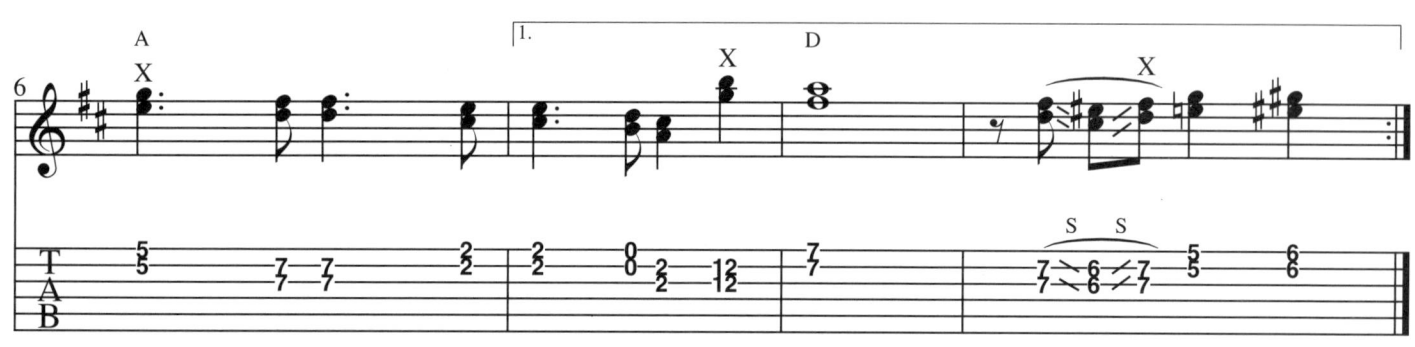

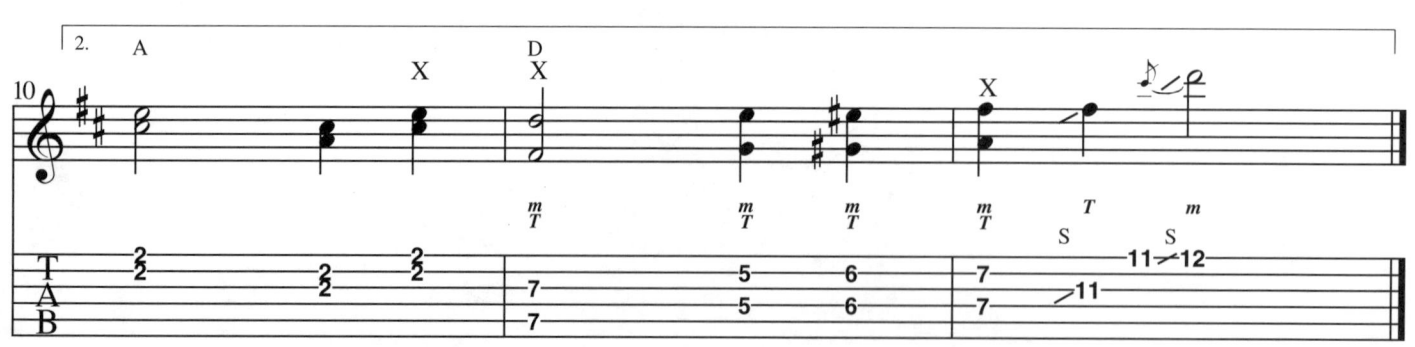

PLAYING "BLUES SHUFFLE IN E"

Next up is a slow blues shuffle in E (page 90). The example below shows one version of the blues scale in G tuning. This scale features the root (1), ♭3, 4, ♭5, 5 and ♭7 scale degrees.

THE E BLUES SCALE

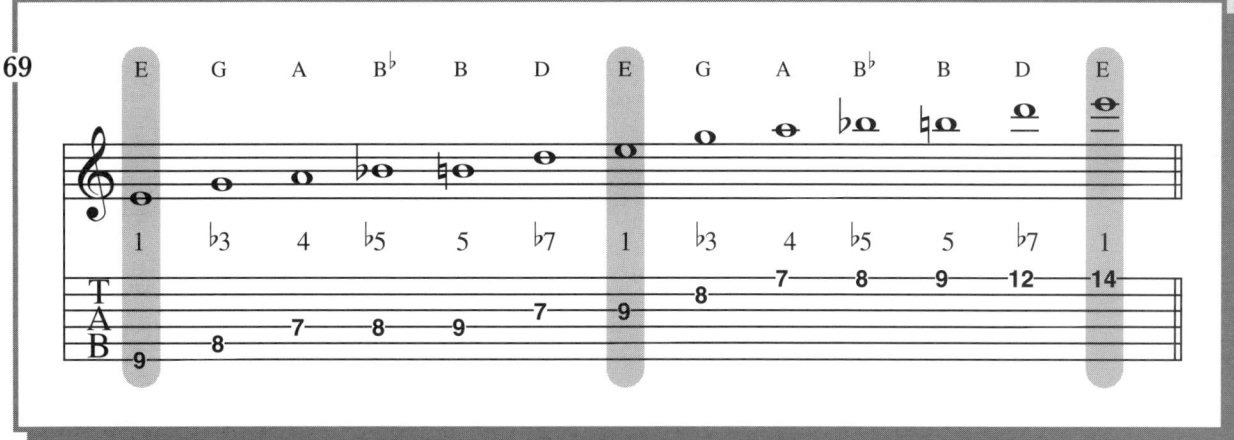

Below is another barring pattern of the E Blues scale, this time shown in a fretboard diagram. The illustration represents the guitar fretboard, with the vertical lines representing the frets and the horizontal lines representing the strings. The top line is the 1st string. The numbers in the dots are the scale degrees of the notes (using the E Major scale). Remember, this is in G tuning.

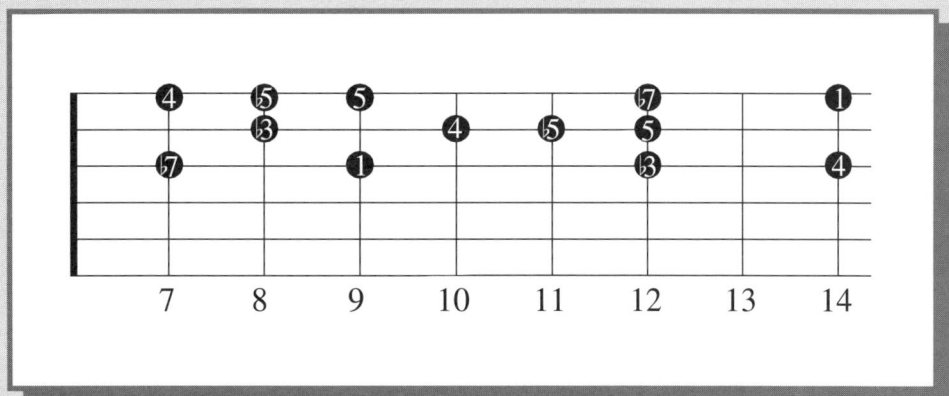

The Multi-Instrumental Guitarist • 89

The next tune employs segments of the E Blues fingering pattern several times. Notice that lots of notes are preceded or followed by slides that don't connect to another specific note. It's up to you how far to slide, but listen to the CD to get an idea of what is typical.

BLUES SHUFFLE IN E

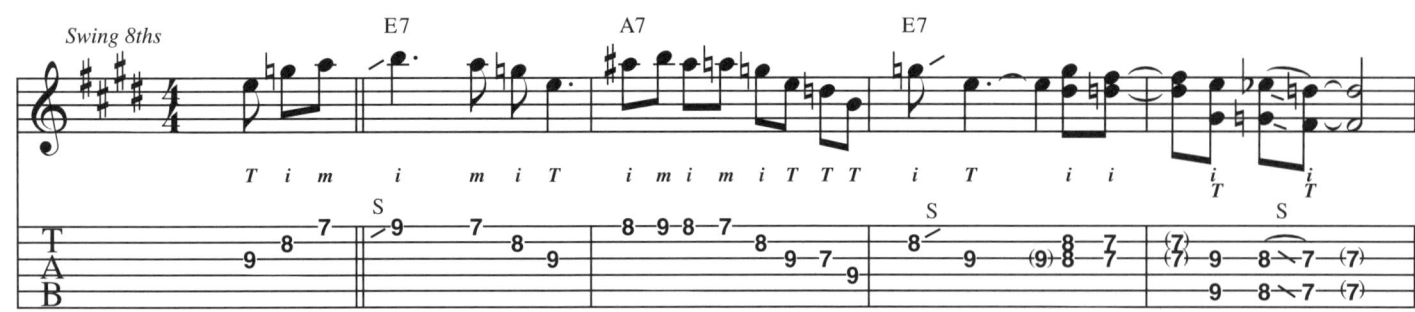

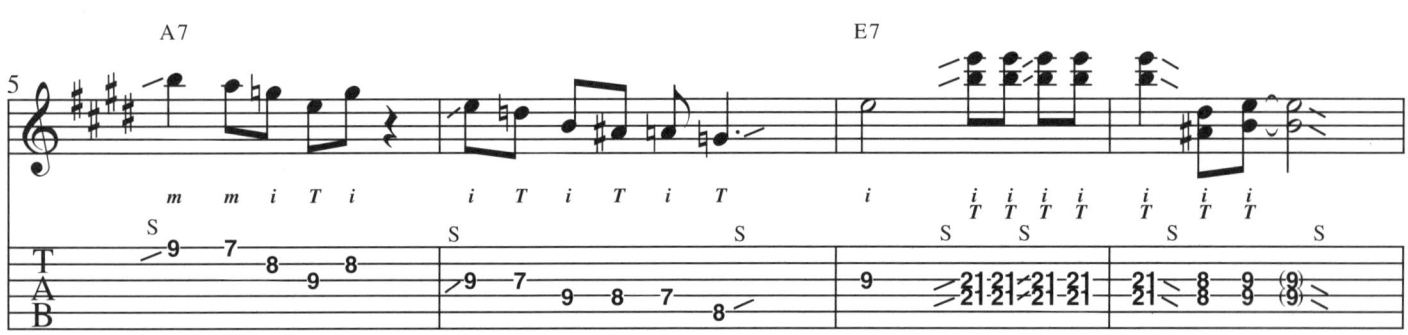

WORKING WITH CHORDS

Playing major chords in high G tuning is about as easy as playing music can get, as demonstrated in "Strumming Blues in D" on page 84. Since the steel guitar is tuned to a major triad, just lay the bar down directly over the desired fret. The open strings and 12th frets are G chords, 1st and 13th frets are G# (or A♭) chords, 2nd and 14th frets are A chords, and so on.

Things get tricky when you want to add embellishments to the triads, but by using combinations of open and closed strings we can ornament certain chords. Below are several examples of dominant and minor chords that no hip steel guitarist should leave home without. On the G7 and E Minor forms, tilt the bar, touching only the 1st, 2nd or 4th string, as indicated (× on a string in the TAB indicates to omit the string.) For the others, lay the bar flat, leaving the indicated strings open.

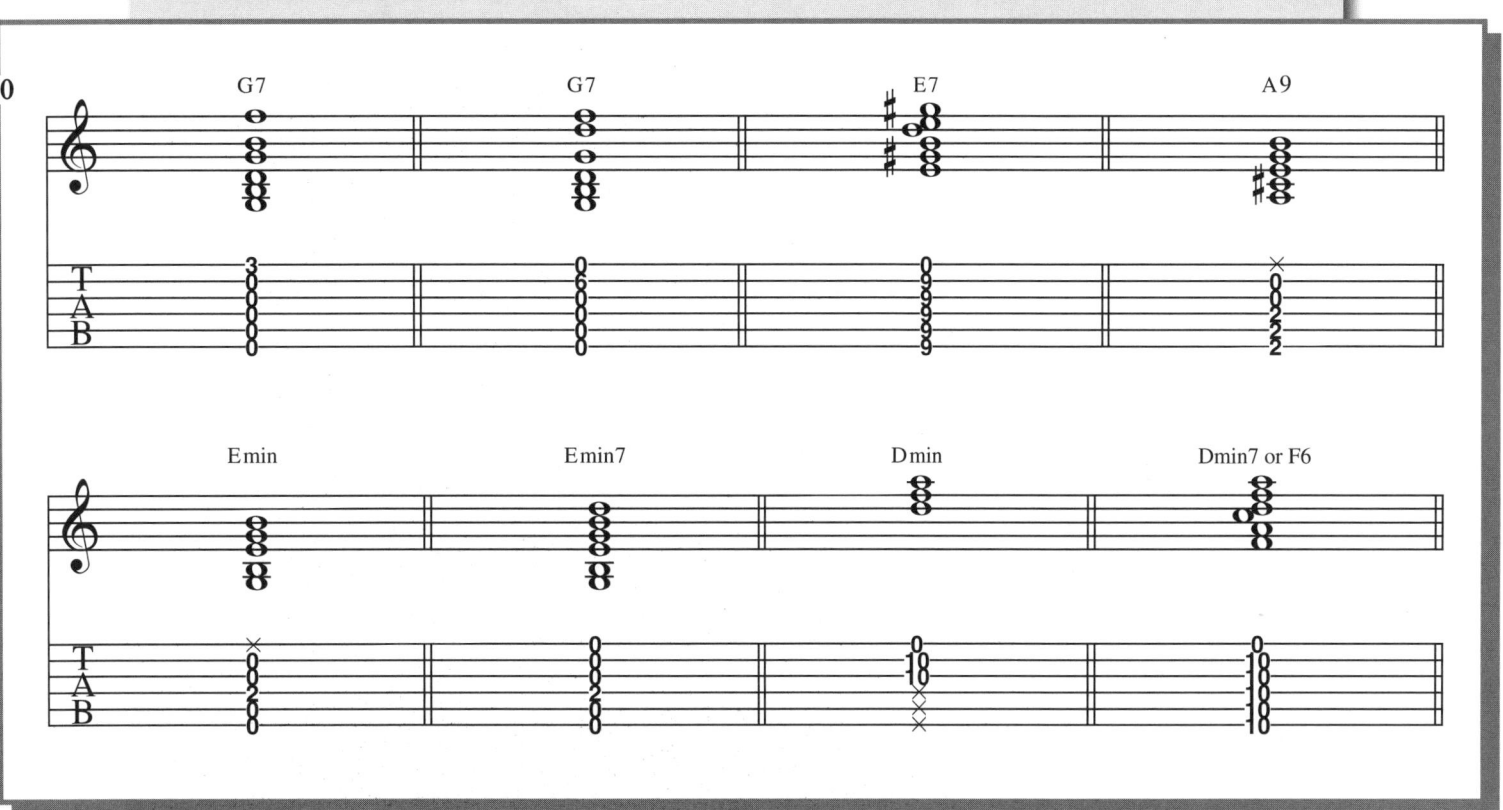

Playing complete forms of most embellished chords may involve such arcane techniques as slanting the bar and pulling the strings from behind the bar, but that's beyond the scope of this book.

When playing in a group situation, the lap guitar is ordinarily not the primary chording instrument. In that circumstance, you can play just a couple of strings at a time as accompaniment. Those pitches can be just the spicy parts of the chords, leaving the rest to band mates to cover. You can think of this approach as approximating what a horn section might do in a blues band.

Below are a few examples, for purposes of illustration, over an E chord. To use the positions on other chords, just shift these up or down the neck to the desired roots. You can use the double stops 5–♭7 and ♭7–9 over dominant chords. The 6–9 double stop is an interesting coloring of a major chord (or on a 6/9 chord). The ♭3–5 double stop is part of a minor chord and a straight position three frets higher than the desired chord gives the ♭3, 5 and ♭7 (for part of a minor 7 chord). Of course, these same double stops can be used as part of a solo instead of as accompaniment; they can also be played an octave lower by moving down three strings.

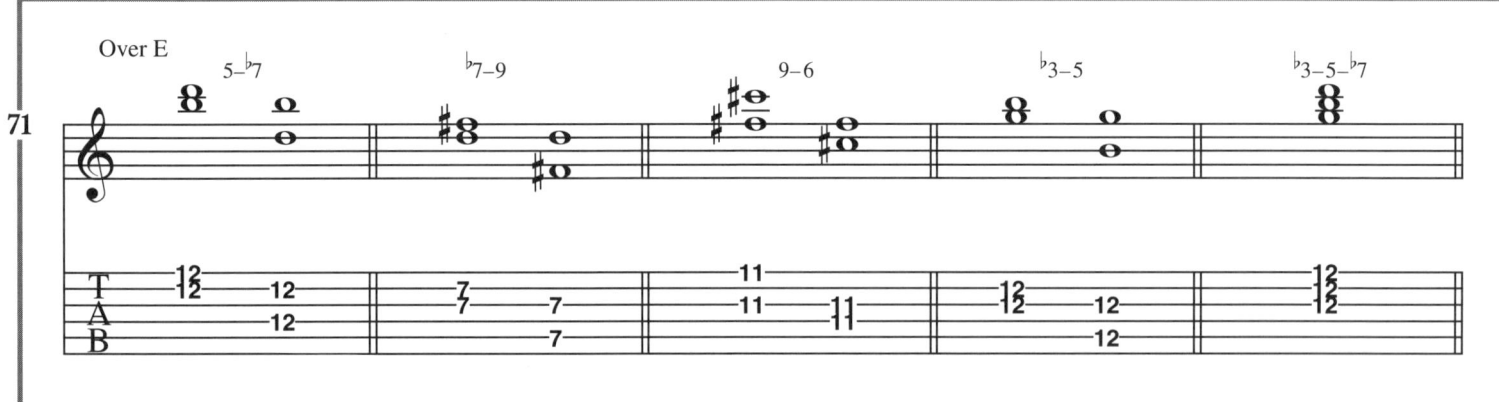

OPEN D TUNING

While second in popularity to G tuning, there are enough players that favor D tuning for blues to warrant a quick look. Here it is:

That makes the intervals between the top two strings the same as tuning for standard tuning (a 4th). Some players will tune this a whole step higher to E. Here the relation to standard tuning is more obvious: E–B–E–G♯–B–E. Tuning a whole step down to a growling C chord is a recent favorite of fellows like David Lindley: C–G–C–E–G–C. For those of an analytic bent, in open D tuning, notice that open strings 2, 3 and 4 are the 5th, 3rd and root notes, of a D Major chord. That is the equivalent of the 1st, 2nd and 3rd strings of the G tuning we have been using. So licks done on strings 1–3 in Open G tuning can be duplicated (in transposed form) on strings 2–4 in Open D tuning.

The next music example illustrates some typical D tuning moves, along with some licks we have already covered in G tuning, now transposed to D tuning. The pickup is similar to the one used in *Country Blues in G* on page 86. In the 3rd measure, the 2nd and 3rd strings on the 8th fret are the ♭7th and 5th of the G7 chord. The same chord tones are shown in G tuning for an E chord in example 71 on page 92. Measures 5 and 6 are a variant of a famous lick from a song called *Dust My Broom* by Elmore James, a riff that almost defines D tuning blues.

PIECE IN OPEN D

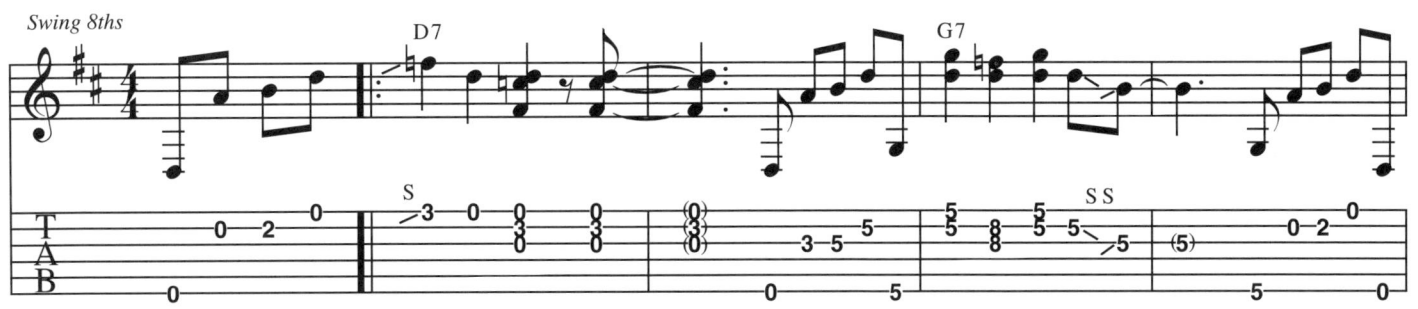
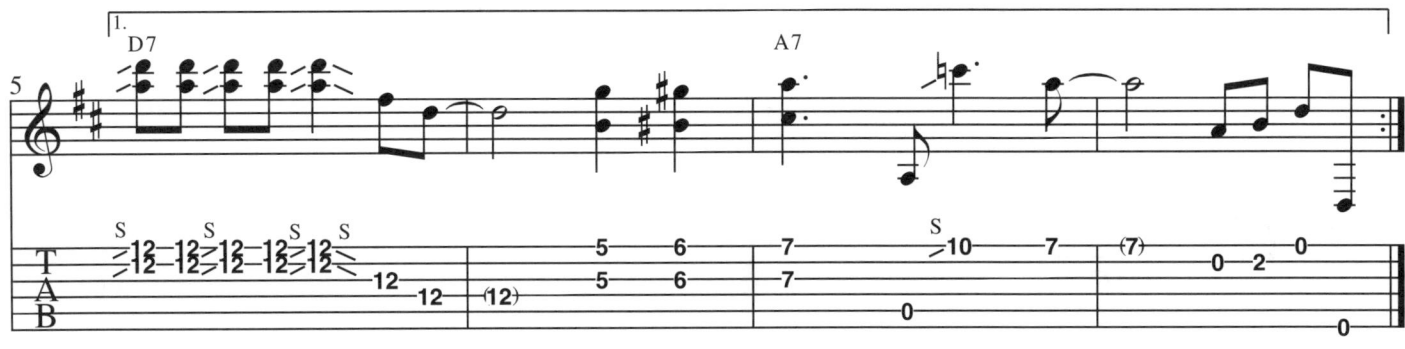
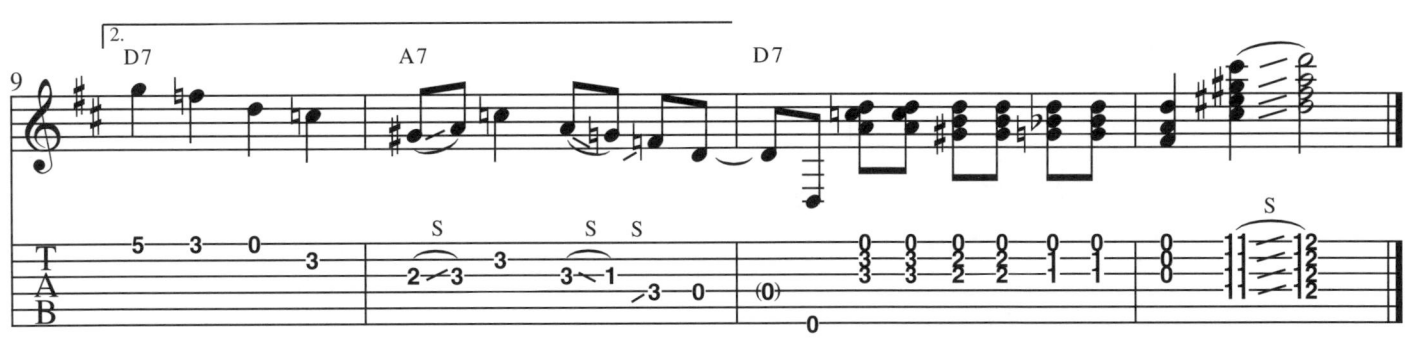

SUMMARY OF TUNINGS

MANDOLIN
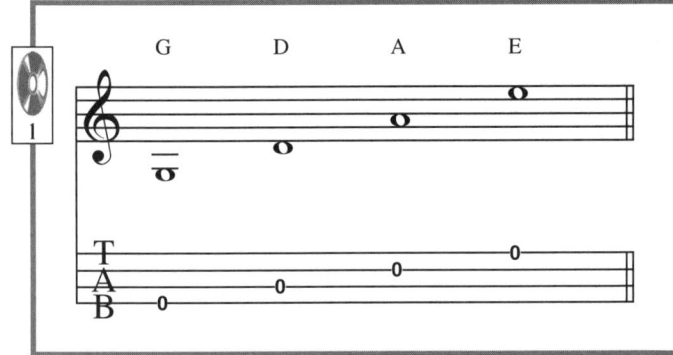

OCTAVE MANDOLIN
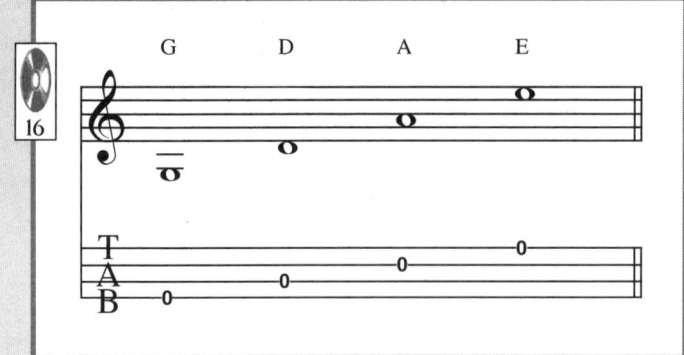

TENOR BANJO
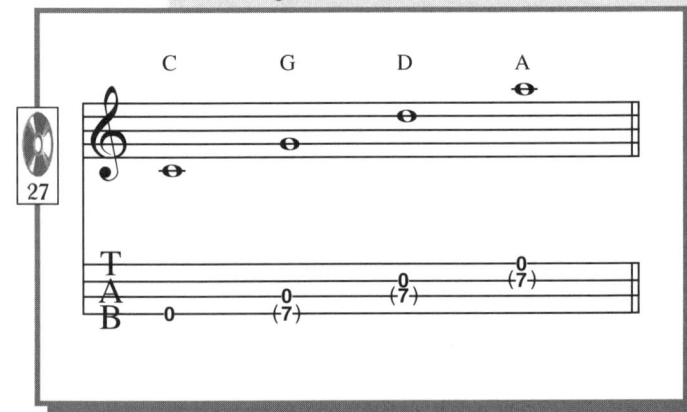

FIVE STRING BANJO—OPEN G
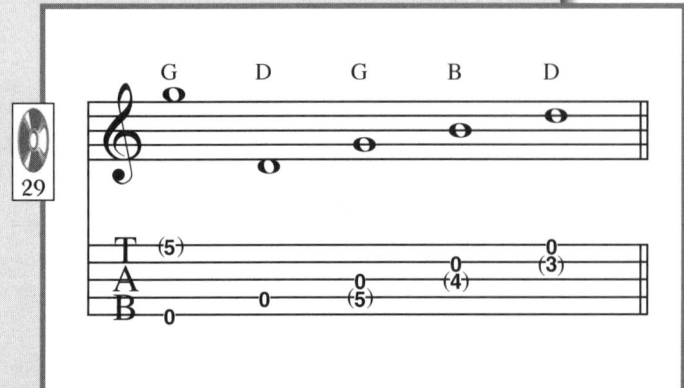

FIVE STRING BANJO—MODAL TUNING
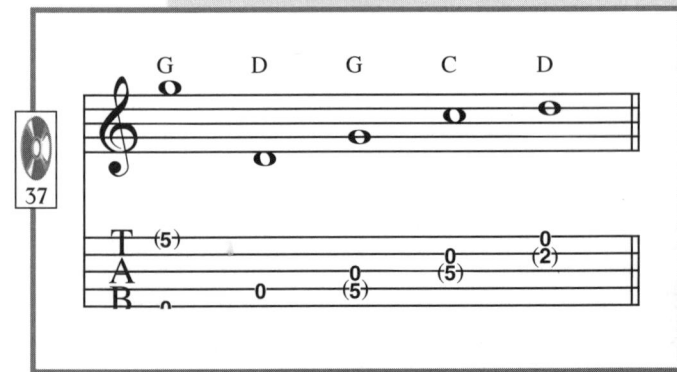

FIVE STRING BANJO—C TUNING
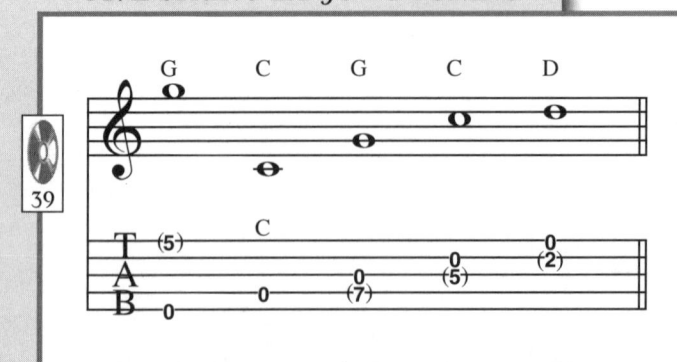

UKULELE TUNING

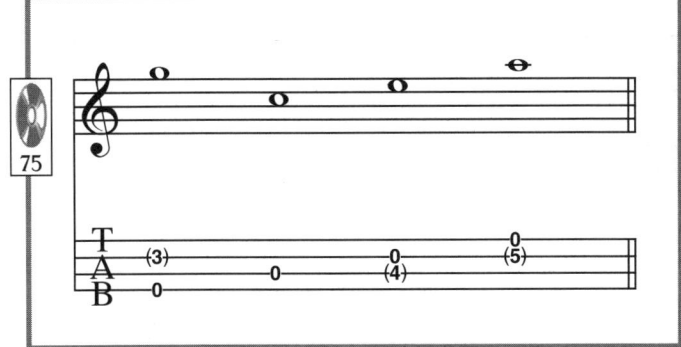

BARITONE UKE AND TENOR GUITAR TUNING

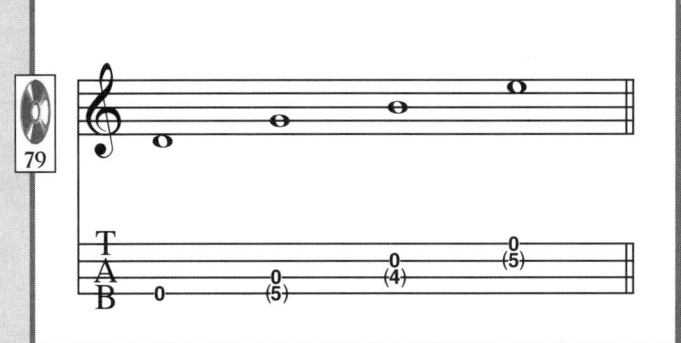

LAP DULCIMER— MIXOLYDIAN TUNING

LAP SLIDE GUITAR— G MAJOR TUNING

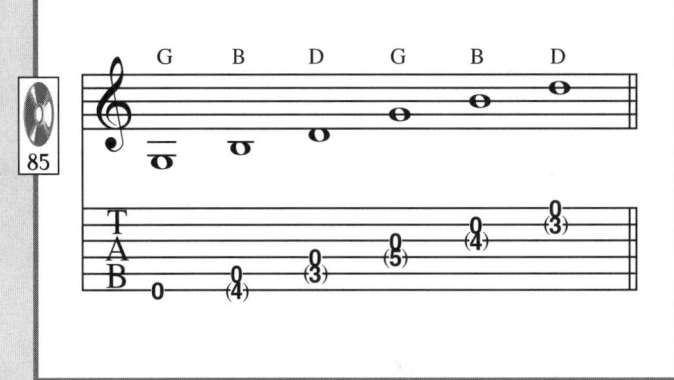

LAP SLIDE GUITAR— OPEN D TUNING

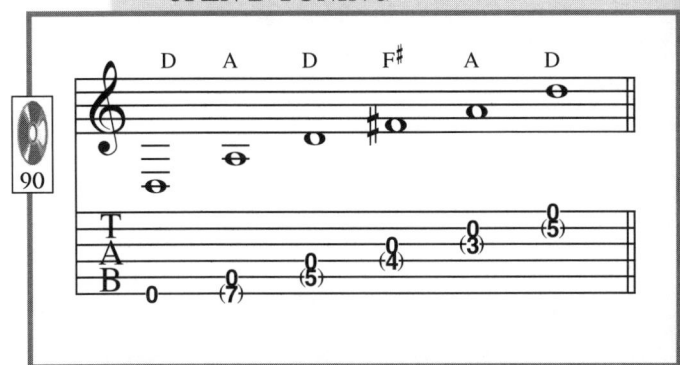

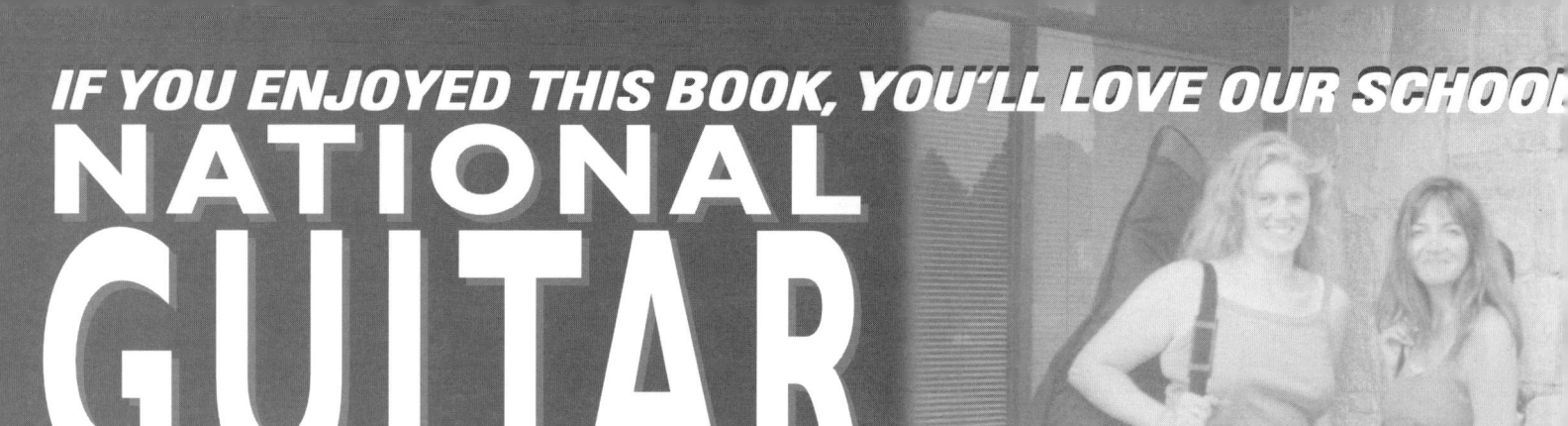